Simple Laotian Cooking

THE HIPPOCRENE
COOKBOOK LIBRARY

Afghan Food & Cookery
African Cooking, Best of Regional
Albanian Cooking, Best of
Argentina Cooks!
Australia, Good Food From
Austrian Cuisine, Best of, Exp. Ed.
Belgian Cookbook, A
Brazilian Cookery, The Art of
Bulgarian Cooking, Traditional
Burma, Flavors of,
Cajun Women, Cooking With
Caucasus Mountains, Cuisines of the
Croatian Cooking, Best of, Exp. Ed.
Czech Cooking, Best of, Exp. Ed.
Danube, All Along The, Exp. Ed.
Dutch Cooking, Art of, Exp. Ed.
Egyptian Cooking
Eritrea, Taste of
Filipino Food, Fine
Finnish Cooking, Best of
French Caribbean Cuisine
French-English Dictionary of
Gastronomic Terms
French Fashion, Cooking in the
(Bilingual)
Greek Cuisine, The Best of, Exp. Ed.
Haiti, Taste of
Havana Cookbook, Old (Bilingual)
Hungarian Cookbook
Hungarian Cooking, Art of, Rev. Ed.
Icelandic Food & Cookery
Indian Spice Kitchen
International Dictionary of
Gastronomy
Irish-Style, Feasting Galore
Italian Cuisine, Treasury of (Bilingual)
Japanese Home Cooking
Korean Cuisine, Best of
Laotian Cooking, Simple
Latvia, Taste of

Lithuanian Cooking, Art of
Mayan Cooking
Mongolian Cooking, Imperial
Norway, Tastes and Tales of
Persian Cooking, Art of
Poland's Gourmet Cuisine
Polish Cooking, Best of, Exp. Ed.
Polish Country Kitchen Cookbook
Polish Cuisine, Treasury of (Bilingual)
Polish Heritage Cookery, Ill. Ed.
Polish Traditions, Old
Portuguese Encounters, Cuisines of
Pyrenees, Tastes of
Quebec, Taste of
Rhine, All Along The
Romania, Taste of, Exp. Ed.
Russian Cooking, Best of, Exp. Ed.
Scandinavian Cooking, Best of
Scotland, Traditional Food From
Scottish-Irish Pub and Hearth
Cookbook
Sephardic Israeli Cuisine
Sicilian Feasts
Slovak Cooking, Best of
Smorgasbord Cooking, Best of
South African Cookery, Traditional
South American Cookery, Art of
South Indian Cooking, Healthy
Spanish Family Cookbook, Rev. Ed.
Sri Lanka, Exotic Tastes of
Swiss Cookbook, The
Syria, Taste of
Taiwanese Cuisine, Best of
Thai Cuisine, Best of, Regional
Turkish Cuisine, Taste of
Ukrainian Cuisine, Best of, Exp. Ed.
Uzbek Cooking, Art of
Wales, Traditional Food From
Warsaw Cookbook, Old

Simple
Laotian
Cooking

Penn Hongthong

HIPPOCRENE BOOKS, INC.
NEW YORK

Book and jacket design by Acme Klong Design, Inc.

For more information, address:
HIPPOCRENE BOOKS, INC.
171 Madison Avenue
New York, NY 10016

ISBN 0-7818-0963-0

Cataloging-in-Publication Data available from the Library of Congress.
Printed in the United States of America.

Table of Contents

Introduction

I grew up in the small town of Paklay, Sayaboury, in the northern part of Laos, a country bordering Vietnam and Thailand. I don't remember at what age I started cooking, but it did become my main task. I shared with my older sister—I am the third oldest and the second girl of nine children—the responsibility of preparing food for the family. My sister would prepare rice and clean the house in the morning while I would go food shopping at the market. Selecting fresh fruits and vegetables, creating new dishes, and planning and cooking the meals for my large family is one of the best memories of growing up in Laos.

In my small town, you had to be at the market by 5:00 A.M. in order to get fresh meat and vegetables. Most of the vendors were farmers selling extra crops, or livestock, and the rest of their day was spent on the rice farms.

My father was a well-known teacher, and my mother managed the convenience store my parents owned in the house. Besides the house chores, I had to help care for my younger brothers and sisters and the store.

I loved going to market because I enjoyed checking the freshness and color of the vegetables and selecting the freshest meats. I had to be creative with cooking, as livestock was limited and fruits and vegetables were seasonal.

Every day pork and chicken were on display, with a selection of vegetables, wild game, and fish that varied daily. Beef was very rare because they were not easy to raise and most were needed to plow the farms. In my town, the meat of water buffalos was occasionally available because they were used to plow the local fields.

To have water buffalo meat the whole town had to gather. There were no refrigerators to store the meat, so each family received large amounts of meat at once. The first night, every family had *lob* for dinner because *lob* requires fresh and lean meat. Some of the meat got salted for the following day's meal, while some got marinated for dried meat, and the rest got smoked and dried to make it last.

Laos is a small, poor, landlocked country. We could not afford to eat a lot of meat, but we were not vegetarians. Meals were prepared with little meat and a

lot of vegetables. I ate a lot of meat during my first couple of months in the United States because it suddenly was readily available. After that I went back to eating the way I used to.

I immigrated to the United States in 1980 when I was 17. My first trip was going to the supermarket. I was amazed by the size and the convenience of shopping carts. Prices were on every item and eggplants and celery branches looked so large that I didn't think they were edible.

My first American meal was roast beef and roasted whole chicken at my sponsor's (we were sponsored by a church) house, where I lived the first six months. I had dreamed of having a meal like that all my life but the meal did not turn out the way I expected. I didn't know that tastes change after vegetables have been refrigerated, meat has been frozen, and tomato sauce has been canned. The worst part was I could not speak or understand a word of English. I couldn't even tell them what was going on.

For many years I did not feel at home and did not like American food. I always wondered why Americans ate so much meat and so few vegetables. However, after so many years, I have come to accept my new home and have learned to like the food. Still, few people are familiar with Laos, so I would like to introduce them to the food I grew up eating and show them how to cook like my mother and grandmothers did in my small town in Laos.

Dairy products like butter, milk, cream, or cheese were unavailable in Laos when I was growing up. The only fat in the food, occasionally, was a little bit of beef or pork fat. Laotian food is cooked with many herbs and spices. One herb or spice can change the taste of the dish completely. Salt is the only thing that goes in every dish. If you don't like the taste of sauces like fish sauce, soy sauce, or oyster sauce, simply omit it and increase the amount of salt. If I didn't list an ingredient, it is because it does not go in that dish. For example, Laotian cooking does not use the black pepper commonly found in American cooking. We also do not oil meats or vegetables before grilling. Some dishes are not supposed to have any oil or fat at all.

A meal is complete with rice, hot sauce, and fresh or steamed vegetable. All meat and vegetable are cut in bite sizes. Food is cooked with a lot of herbs and spices to make it flavorful and salty, in order to serve dishes with plain rice. Noodles are made from rice flour only, and served occasionally.

Since there were no ovens in Laos, most foods were cooked in a pot, barbecued, steamed, or roasted in banana leaves over fire. Pork fat was used for stir-frying and deep-frying, and it was expensive because it came from an animal. Vegetable oil was imported, which made it expensive, so most of the cooking was done without oil. Older people prefer nonfried food. My dearest grandmother did not eat any stir-fried or fried food and had very little meat.

Desserts, though rare, were always made with coconut milk, and fried or steamed. Fresh fruits after a meal were more common. In the afternoon, instead of getting together to have tea, coffee, and dessert, Laotian women got together to have sour fruits or papaya salad.

Water was the only drink at home. We did not have the luxury of having juice and soda in the refrigerator like in the United States. If we ate out, we might have had fresh coconut juice, fresh sugar cane juice, iced tea with no sugar, iced coffee, and tropical fruit juices made of blended fresh fruits and ice without sugar.

Each recipe indicates exactly what you can substitute. Spanish stores sell many ingredients you might need, such as coconut, coconut milk, coconut cream, coconut juice, cilantro, mint, papaya, dried tamarind, banana leaves, taro root, yucca root, and mango.

Have fun shopping and cooking.

Surn sap
(*Enjoy your meal*)

Glossary

Asian squash

Asian squash has a soft taste almost like cucumber. It makes a light soup and is great for sautés. You can also steam it and serve with steamed fish in banana leaves.

Bamboo shoots

Bamboo shoots exist in many different sizes and shapes. Use only as directed, fresh, canned, or dried.

Basil

Basil must be used fresh. Thai basil (or cinnamon basil) has a stronger flavor than Italian basil, but use either one. Many nurseries sell basil plants.

Chayote

Chayote is sold in many supermarkets. It is great in soup, sautéed, and steamed. It has a light and slightly sweet taste.

Cilantro

Cilantro must be used fresh. It is available in many supermarkets. It is sometimes called Chinese parsley or coriander, and is not the same as curly parsley or Italian flat-leaf parsley. It is an acquired taste for some people.

Coconut

Coconut juice is the clear water from inside the coconut, and is for drinking. Coconut milk is a blend of water and coconut meat that has been squeezed and strained. Cream of coconut is coconut milk sweetened with sugar.

Dill

Dill is only used fresh. It has a very strong flavor that does not go well with everything. Be careful not to let it get in a dish that is not suppose to have it; a little bit will change the taste of the dish. Dill is sold in almost every supermarket.

Eggplant

Any kind of eggplant will work fine; the smaller the size the better the taste. They grow in many varieties, sizes, and colors. Some are crispy and can be served raw.

Ginger

Ginger is always used fresh. Practically every supermarket sells fresh ginger as a knobby root. Buy just enough to use for one time. If you buy too much, make sure the outside is dry, leave on the counter overnight, wrap with paper towels, and store in a plastic bag in the refrigerator. Check every week. If it is too moist, change the paper towel and open the bag; if it is too dry, close the bag. Ginger must be cut across the grain before being julienned or blended for marinades, because it is very fibrous.

Kaffir lime leaves

Kaffir lime leaves can be used fresh, frozen, or dried. If you do a lot of Laotian cooking, it is best to have a tree, as most Laotians do. Grow it in a pot that you'll take outside in summer and bring inside in winter. It needs a lot of sun. Do not confuse kaffir lime leaves with lime, orange and grapefruit leaves. They look identical but the latter ones are not edible.

Kalanga (galangal)

Kalanga is a type of ginger, but it is harder and tastes different from ginger. Dried kalanga is used only for soup. For other dishes, use the fresh, frozen, or powdered kind. If it is not available, omit it, do not substitute with ginger.

Lemon basil

Lemon basil has a very different taste than other basil varieties. Laotians call it *puck e to* and Thais call it *mang luck*. Do not substitute with other kinds of basil. If it is not available, omit it.

Lemongrass

Dried lemongrass is best for soup; it is too hard for other uses. Most gourmet and specialty stores sell fresh lemongrass. If you buy it fresh, cut it 3 or 4 inches long, store in a plastic bag, and freeze it for later. Lemongrass is very fibrous, so slice it thinly across the grain and blend well in a blender before using in marinades. In Laos, it grows wild and is very inexpensive. In the United States, some nurseries sell potted lemongrass that you can grow yourself. It is easy to grow but needs a lot of sun.

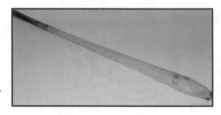

Mint

Mint must be used fresh. Spearmint has a stronger flavor than other mints. It is easy to grow and comes back every year (perennial).

Papaya

Use green or hard yellow papayas to make salad. When a ripe papaya turns orange and soft, have it as a fruit after a meal. There are many varieties of papayas in Laos, ranging from half a pound to 20 pounds. They grow on trees 3 to 25 feet tall.

Pepper

Hot peppers come in many different sizes: the smaller the size the hotter they are. If you like your dishes hot and someone else does not, add ground or chopped hot pepper to your own plate. Add whole small peppers while cooking, but be careful to not overcook them. If you like it super hot, chop chili peppers in a food processor, store in an airtight container, and freeze. Add the desired amount to your food.

Shallot

Shallot can be substituted with onion, but you will have to use more because shallot has more flavor than onion. Shallots are used a lot in Laotian cooking. Onions do not grow very big in Laos.

Tamarind

Tamarind is a sour fruit that can be used fresh, dried, or juiced. It is substituted with lime juice, lemon juice, ketchup and sometimes vinegar. There are two kinds of tamarinds in Laos: sweet and sour. When they are young, they are all green and sour, so Laotians eat them as sour fruits. When they are ripe, the sweet ones turn sweet while the sour ones stay sour. Both green and ripe can be used but in different dishes. They grow in very large trees up to 8 feet wide and 40 feet tall.

Tofu

Tofu is not used a lot in Laos; it is from China. But because it has a lot of proteins, I try to use as much as possible. Since it is essentially flavorless and absorbs the taste of whatever it is mixed with, sneak it in any dish that you cook.

Watercress

Watercress tastes a little bitter and adds great taste to a salad. However, its bitterness disappears in a second when it is cooked. It is very good as a light soup. In Laos, they grow in the sandy and rocky soil on the side of small streams. They are not very abundant so their price is in the medium range.

Winter melon

Winter melon becomes clear after cooking. It makes for very light and refreshing soups. They weigh from 1 to 30 pounds, and grow on vines like pumpkins. They can be used young or old, as they taste the same. Young ones last for a couple of weeks while the old ones last many months if not cut.

Appetizers

Crepes Stuffed with Bean Sprouts and Pork

BUN SAIL

2 cups flour	2 cups fresh bean sprouts
2 large eggs	1 teaspoon salt
1 tablespoon yellow curry powder	2 stalks scallions, chopped
½ pound ground pork or turkey	1 tablespoon vegetable oil

In a large mixing bowl, add flour, 1½ cups water, eggs, and curry. Mix well and set aside.

Place ground pork in nonstick pan and cook on medium heat. Stir occasionally and cook 8 minutes. Turn the heat to high for a minute to reduce all the juice from the meat. Let cool 10 minutes. Transfer to a food processor and chop 10 seconds. Transfer to a large mixing bowl and set aside.

Heat the same pan in which you cooked the pork on high heat. Add bean sprouts and stir constantly 2 minutes. Keep the heat high to reduce the water from the sprouts but do not overcook. Add salt and scallions, stir well, and turn off the heat. Transfer to the pork, mix well, and set aside.

Heat a clean nonstick pan on medium heat and brush lightly with oil. Pour in ⅓ cup batter. Pick up the pan and twirl to cover the bottom of the pan. Place the pan back on the burner, cover, and cook 2 minutes. Add a spoonful of the pork mixture on one side of the crepe. Use a spatula to pick up the other end and fold over the mixture. Cover and cook 30 seconds. Turn it over to cook the other side for another 30 seconds.

Serve hot with Peanut Sauce (page 60).

SERVES 4

Crispy Noodles

4 cups vegetable oil	$\frac{1}{2}$ teaspoon salt
4 ounces dried rice noodles	2 tablespoons fish sauce
	2 tablespoons tamarind juice
SAUCE:	1 stalk scallion, chopped
3 tablespoons olive oil	$\frac{1}{2}$ cup chopped cilantro
$\frac{1}{2}$ pound shrimp, peeled and	1 cup fresh bean sprouts
cleaned	$\frac{1}{4}$ cup julienned fresh red bell pepper
$\frac{1}{4}$ cup plus 2 tablespoons	
granulated sugar	

Heat the vegetable oil in a wok or a medium pan on high heat. Add 1 ounce rice noodles at a time (they will immediately puff up). Turn it over with tongs to fry the other side and immediately take the noodles out and place on paper towels to absorb the oil. Repeat with the remaining noodles and set aside.

FOR THE SAUCE: Heat a wok with the oil on high heat. Add shrimp and stir constantly 1 minute. Take the shrimp out and set aside, leaving the oil in the wok. Add $\frac{1}{4}$ cup sugar, and caramelize until light brown. Add 2 tablespoons sugar, salt, fish sauce, and tamarind juice. Stir well and cook until thickened, 5 minutes. Add the shrimp back in, stir well, and cook another minute. Let cool 5 minutes.

Transfer the noodles to an extra large mixing bowl. Add one spoon of mixture at a time to the noodles. Mix lightly with both hands until the noodles are coated with the mixture. Add the scallion and cilantro and mix lightly. Transfer to a serving plate.

Garnish with bean sprouts around the noodles. Sprinkle with red pepper and serve at room temperature.

SERVES 6

Fresh Spring Rolls

YALL DIP

This dish is very healthful and great for vegetarians when prepared without the shrimp. It's a great dish to serves in the summer when the weather is hot and you don't want to add any heat in the house; just buy cooked shrimp and wrap it up. My family makes this dish almost every time we get together. The best time to make this dish is in the spring, when the mint leaves are young and fresh. These rolls always remind me of spring.

3 ounces somen noodles (optional)	1 cup fresh bean sprouts
1 pound shrimp, peeled and cooked, 1 pound ground pork or turkey, or marinated tofu, sliced	1 cup cilantro leaves
	1 cup mint leaves
1 cup mesclun or any other type of lettuce	1 package (25 pieces) dried rice paper

Bring 3 cups water to a boil on high heat. Add noodles, stir well, and turn the heat to medium. Cook 3 minutes. Rinse with cold water and drain well in a strainer for 30 minutes.

If using ground pork or turkey, add the meat to a nonstick wok or pan. Cook on medium heat and stir constantly until dried, 8 minutes (do not brown). Let cool 5 minutes.

Transfer to a food processor and chop 20 seconds, then set aside.

GET READY TO ROLL: Line up bowls of cooked shrimp or meat, noodles, sprouts, mesclun, cilantro, mint, and large bowl of hot water from faucet (change water as it gets cool).

Continued

Line up 3 large plates. Dip one sheet of rice paper in water for 5 seconds, hold up to let the excess water drip out, 5 seconds. Carefully place it flat on a large plate. Repeat for 2 more times. Wait for a minute to allow the paper to get soft. The first paper should be ready to roll (as you finish rolling each one, dip another paper).

On the end near you, place 2 shrimp, 3 tablespoons of noodles, 4 mesclun leaves, 10 bean sprouts, 6 cilantro leaves, and 4 mint leaves. Fold over the end near you, roll over once, fold 2 sides toward each other, hold it tight, and roll over toward the other end.

NOTE: Since the paper is made from rice, it will stick to itself. Remember not to put in too much filling because you will not be able to roll it nicely.

Serve with Peanut Sauce (page 60).

SERVES 6

Fried Spring Rolls

YALL JEUNE

Fried spring rolls must be rolled and fried or frozen immediately after mixing. Do not mix and refrigerate overnight. They will turn sour. When making ahead of time, lay each roll on a tray and place wax paper between each layer. Place plastic wrap on top when finished and cover. Freeze until ready to use (do not thaw). Fry on medium heat. It will taste as good as fresh.

½ cup dried wood ear mushrooms (optional)	3 large eggs
1 package (1.7 ounces) cellophane noodles	2 teaspoons salt
	2 tablespoons soy sauce
1 pound ground pork or turkey	1½ tablespoons sugar
1 small onion, chopped	1½ teaspoons ground black pepper
1 cup shredded carrot	1 package (25 pieces) frozen spring roll wrappers, thawed
2 cups bean sprouts	6 cups vegetable oil

Soak wood ears in hot water for 45 minutes, drain well, and then chop. Soak cellophane noodles in warm water 10 minutes, drain well, and cut in segments 4 inches long.

In a large mixing bowl, add wood ears, noodles, pork, onion, carrot, bean sprouts, 2 of the eggs, salt, soy sauce, sugar, and black pepper. Mix well with both hands (use gloves if desired).

Mix the remaining egg in a small bowl for gluing. Place one wrapper on a flat surface, pointing one corner at you. Brush the opposite corner with egg wash. Spoon 4 tablespoons of the mixture on the corner near you. Fold that corner over, roll it over just once, fold over left and right corners, and continue rolling all the way toward the far. The egg wash will glue the roll together. Repeat until finished.

Heat oil in a frying pan on medium-high heat. Fry the spring rolls until golden brown, 5 minutes on each side. Place on paper towels to absorb the excess oil.

Serve hot by itself or with Peanut Sauce (page 60) or Plum Sauce (page 61).

SERVES 6

Fried Wonton

JEUNE WONTON

The fried garlic and onion add a sweet taste to this mixture, and give the oil extra flavor. You can add some chopped shrimp for better taste or ground turkey for less fat.

Wontons can be made ahead of time. Lay each wonton on a tray and place wax paper between each layer. Place plastic wrap on top when finished and cover. Freeze until ready to use (do not thaw). Fried on medium heat, they will taste as good as fresh.

½ cup dried wood ear mushrooms (optional)	1 teaspoon salt
4 cups vegetable oil	1 teaspoon ground black pepper
1 head garlic, peeled	2 tablespoons soy sauce
1 medium onion, sliced	1 tablespoon sugar
1 pound ground pork, turkey, or shrimp	1 package (50 pieces) wonton wrappers
	1 egg yolk

Soak wood ears in hot water for 45 minutes, drain well, and mince.

Heat oil in large frying pan or wok on high heat. Add garlic and onion and stir constantly until golden brown. Transfer to paper towels to absorb oil. Reserve the oil to fry the wontons. Turn off the heat until you are finished wrapping the wonton.

Combine garlic and onion in a food processor and chop 10 seconds. Add mushrooms, ground pork, salt, pepper, soy sauce, and sugar and chop another 10 seconds. Transfer to a mixing bowl and mix well.

Place 1 wonton skin on a plate. Mix yolk in a small bowl. Brush the egg along the sides. Spoon 1 tablespoon of the pork mixture on the center of the skin. Bring 1 corner to the other corner to make a triangle. Press edges to seal. Repeat until finished.

Reheat the reserved oil on medium high. When the oil gets hot, drop in wontons, one at a time and fry until golden brown, about 5 minutes or drop in boiling water and cook 5 minutes. Place on paper towels to absorb the oil and serve hot.

SERVES 6

Skewered Chicken

SATAY

1 pound boneless chicken breast	¼ teaspoon ground white pepper
½ tablespoon yellow curry powder	10 bamboo sticks, soaked in water
½ teaspoon salt	overnight or at least 2 hours
1½ teaspoon sugar	3 tablespoon coconut milk
1½ teaspoon fish sauce	
1½ teaspoon soy sauce	

Cut each chicken breast into 5 strips and place in a medium mixing bowl. Add curry, salt, sugar, fish sauce, soy sauce, pepper, and coconut milk. Mix well, cover and refrigerate overnight or at least 2 hours.

Skewer bamboo sticks though chicken strips lengthwise. Grill each side 5 minutes or broil in oven 8 minutes each side. Serve hot with warm Satay Sauce (page 62).

SERVES 4

Soups

Asian Squash Soup

GANG MOCK NUM

1 pound young Asian squash	2 teaspoons salt
2 or 3 pounds pork neck bones or	2 stalks scallions, chopped
chicken bones	1/2 cup chopped cilantro

Peel the Asian squash and cut into 1/2-inch cubes (do not seed).

In a medium pot add 8 cups water and bring to a boil. Add the bones and return to a boil. Cover and simmer 45 minutes. The broth will reduce to 4 cups.

After simmering, discard the bones. Let the broth cool, strain, and drain the fat. Transfer to a clean pot and bring to a boil. Add squash and salt, stir well, and bring to a boil. Cook 3 minutes. Add scallion, stir well, and turn off the heat. Add cilantro and serve hot.

SERVES 4

Bamboo Soup

GANG NALL MIKE

I love lemon basil. My paternal grandmother grew a lot of it. I always think of her when I smell lemon basil. If you don't have lemon basil leaves for this dish, omit them. Do not substitute another kind of basil. They do not have the same taste. When choosing bamboo, chose whole ones and slice them yourself because the pre-sliced ones are too small.

In season, Laotian women get together and make a large pot of bamboo shoot soup to have for lunch.

¼ cup uncooked rice	1 small zucchini, cut in bite-size
1 ear fresh corn	pieces
1 hot pepper (optional)	1 cup fresh button mushrooms,
1 can (20 ounces) whole bamboo,	halved
sliced	3.5 ounces oyster mushrooms
1 can (12.85 ounces) yanang leaf	3.5 ounces enoki mushrooms
extract	1 teaspoon salt
1 stalk lemongrass, smashed and	3 tablespoons fish sauce (optional)
cut in 4-inch pieces	1 cup lemon basil leaves (optional)
1 cup cubed buttercup squash	

Soak the rice in warm water for 30 minutes.

Slice the kernels from the ear of corn and set aside.

In a blender, add rice, pepper, and ¼ cup water. Blend 10 seconds and set aside.

In a large pot, bring to a boil 4 cups water, bamboo, yanang leaf extract, and lemongrass. Add pumpkin and corn. Cover and cook 5 minutes. Add zucchini, button, oyster, and enoki mushrooms, blended rice, salt, and fish sauce. Stir well, cover, and cook 3 minutes. Add basil leaves and turn off the heat.

Serve with sticky rice and hot sauce for a meal.

SERVES 4

Bok Choy and Tofu Soup

GANG TAO HOO PUCK GOT KAO

2 or 3 pounds pork neck bones or chicken bones 2 teaspoons salt ½ package (7.5 ounces) tofu, cut in ¼-inch cubes	½ pound bok choy, chopped 2 stalks scallions, chopped

In a medium pot add 8 cups water and bring to a boil. Add the bones and bring to a boil. Turn the heat low, cover, and simmer 45 minutes. The broth will reduce to 4 cups.

After simmering, discard the bones. Let the broth cool, strain, and drain fat.

Transfer to a clean pot and bring to a boil. Add salt and tofu and stir well. Cook 5 minutes. Add bok choy, stir well, and bring to a boil. Turn off the heat, and add scallions, stirring well. Serve hot.

SERVES 4

Cellophane Noodle Soup

GANG SEN RORN

1 cup dried bamboo shoots	2 teaspoons salt
½ cup dried wood ear mushrooms	1 tablespoon soy sauce
1 cup dried lily flowers	2 stalks scallions, chopped
1 package (1.7 ounces) cellophane	½ cup chopped cilantro
noodles	½ teaspoon ground white pepper
1 pound boneless chicken breast	

Soak bamboo shoots in hot water for 45 minutes and cut in 1-inch lengths.

Soak wood ear in hot water for 45 minutes and slice.

Soak dried lily in warm water for 15 minutes and make a knot in each flower.

Soak cellophane noodles in warm water for 15 minutes and cut them in 4-inch lengths.

In a large pot, bring 6 cups water to a boil on high heat. Add chicken and salt, bring to a boil, turn the heat to medium, cover, and cook 15 minutes. Take out the chicken, let cool, and shred.

Continue boiling the broth. Add bamboo, keep the heat on medium, cover, and cook 15 minutes. Turn the heat high, add wood ears and flowers and cook 5 minutes. Add noodles, soy sauce, and chicken, stir well, and bring to a boil. Add scallions, stir well, and turn off the heat. Add cilantro and white pepper and serve hot.

SERVES 8

Chicken Bamboo Soup

GANG GICE NALL MIKE

A great variety of bamboo is available. For this dish, choose fat and short canned bamboo.

1 can (13.5 ounces) whole bamboo	2 stalks scallions, cut in
1 pound boneless chicken breast,	1-inch-long pieces
cut in bite-size pieces	2 tablespoons lime juice
2 teaspoons salt	

Rinse and cut the bamboo in bite-size pieces, 1 inch long and ½ inch thick.

In a medium pot add 4 cups water and bring to a boil. Add chicken and salt. Cook 3 minutes. Add bamboo, bring to a boil, and cook 3 minutes. Add scallions and turn off the heat. Add lime juice before serving.

Serve hot with Sweet and Sour Sauce (page 64) and rice for a light meal.

SERVES 4

Chicken Cabbage Soup

GANG GALUM

This soup is quick and tasty.

1 pound chicken breast, cut in bite-size pieces	1 large firm ripe tomato, cut in ½-inch cubes
2 teaspoons salt	2 stalks scallions, chopped
1 pound green cabbage, cut in bite-size pieces	

In a medium pot, bring 4 cups water to a boil on high heat. Add chicken and salt, and cook 5 minutes. Add cabbage and bring to a boil. Add tomato and scallions, stir well, and turn off the heat.

Serve as soup or with rice and hot sauce as quick meal.

SERVES 2 TO 4

Chicken Coconut Soup

GICE TOME KA

I always try to add tofu into meals. It is a delicious addition to this soup. If using dried lemongrass, wrap it in cheese cloth and discard before serving.

4 slices fresh or dried kalanga	1 teaspoon salt
½ stalk fresh lemongrass, cut in 2-inch pieces across the grain or 2 tablespoons dried (optional)	2 tablespoons fish sauce
	5 ounces fresh button mushrooms, sliced
2 kaffir lime leaves (optional)	1 stalk scallion, chopped
1 can (13.5 ounces) coconut milk	½ cup chopped cilantro
1 pound boneless chicken breast, sliced in bite-size pieces	
½ package (7.5 ounces) tofu, cut in ¼-inch cubes	

In a medium pot, add 6 cups water, kalanga, lemongrass and kaffir lime leaves. Bring to a boil, cover, and simmer 45 minutes. It will reduce to 4 cups.

Turn the heat to high, add coconut milk, and bring to a boil. Add chicken, tofu, salt, and fish sauce. Cook 5 minutes. Add mushrooms, bring to a boil, and turn off the heat. Add scallion and stir well. Add cilantro before serving.

SERVES 6

Chicken Ginger Soup

GANG SOME GICE

The combination of lime juice and ginger in this soup will refresh you from fatigue and nausea. Your energy will perk when you take a spoonful of soup and a bite of chicken dipped in ginger sauce. It always works for me.

3 large boneless chicken breasts	1 stalk scallion, chopped
2 inches fresh ginger, sliced in 6 pieces	½ cup chopped cilantro
3 teaspoons salt	4 tablespoons lime juice

Cut each chicken breast across the grain in 4 pieces.

In a medium pot add 6 cups water and ginger, bring to a boil and simmer 10 minutes. Add chicken and salt. Cover and cook 8 minutes. Turn off the heat and add the scallion. Add cilantro and lime juice before serving.

Serve hot with Ginger Sauce (page 58) and rice for a quick and easy meal.

SERVES 2

Chicken Green Tomato Soup

GANG GICE MOCK LENT DIP

Lemon basil is sold in Thai and Laotian grocery stores. You can also grow it yourself. If not available, omit. Do not substitute with any other kind of basil, which have different flavors. Thais call it *mang luck*, while Laotians call it *puck e too*. Green tomato has a soft sour taste that, paired with lemon basil, brings out an exotic aroma and taste. Give it a try, you will find it interesting.

1 pound boneless chicken breast, cut in bite-size pieces	2 stalks scallions, cut in 1-inch-long pieces
3 teaspoons salt	1 cup lemon basil leaves
2 medium green tomatoes, cut in ½-inch cubes	

In a medium pot, bring 6 cups water to a boil. Add chicken and salt. Cover and cook 5 minutes. Add tomatoes, bring to a boil, and turn off the heat. Add scallions and lemon basil leaves and stir well.

Serve hot with rice and hot sauce for a light meal.

SERVES 4

Chicken Mushroom Soup

TOME SOUP GICE

1 inch fresh ginger, sliced across the grain in 4 pieces	2 kaffir lime leaves (optional)
1 stalk fresh lemongrass, cut in 2-inch pieces across the grain or 2 tablespoons dried (optional)	1 large chicken breast
	1 teaspoon salt
	10 ounces button mushrooms, quartered
6 cloves garlic	2 tablespoons fish sauce
3 shallots or 1 small onion, sliced	1 stalk scallion, chopped
1 large green hot pepper or ¼ bell pepper for a non-spicy dish	½ cup chopped cilantro

Preheat oven to broil.

On a roasting pan place ginger, lemongrass, garlic, shallots, and pepper. Broil 8 minutes on each side and let cool 5 minutes.

In a medium pot, add 8 cups water, ginger, lemongrass, and kaffir lime leaves. Bring to a boil on high heat. Add chicken and salt, cook 10 minutes. Take the chicken out and let cool. Continue to simmer the broth another 30 minutes.

Chop the garlic, shallots, and pepper and shred the chicken. Turn the heat to high and add mushrooms, garlic, shallots, pepper, and fish sauce. Stir well, cover, and bring to a boil. Add chicken and stir well. Bring to a boil and turn off the heat. Add scallion and stir well. Add cilantro before serving.

SERVES 6

Chayote Soup

GANG MOCK NOY THAI

Chayote does not grow well in Laos and is expensive there. You can prepare it in soups, or try it sautéed or steamed as a side vegetable. It has a nice sweet taste.

2 or 3 pounds pork neck bones or chicken bones	2 teaspoons salt
1 medium chayote	1 stalk scallion, chopped
	½ cup chopped cilantro

In a medium pot, bring 8 cups water to a boil. Add the bones and bring to a boil.

Cover and simmer 45 minutes. The broth will reduce to 4 cups.

While the bones are simmering, peel and seed the chayote. Cut into ¼-inch pieces and soak in cold water until ready to use.

After simmering, discard the bones, and let the broth cool. Strain and drain fat.

Transfer to a clean pot and bring to a boil. Add salt and chayote and cook 5 minutes. Turn off the heat and add scallion. Add cilantro before serving.

SERVES 4

Cucumber Soup

GANG MOCK TANG

MEATBALLS:	SOUP:
½ pound ground pork	1 pound Kirby cucumber
1 teaspoon garlic powder	1 teaspoon salt
½ teaspoon ground black pepper	1 stalk scallion, chopped
½ teaspoon salt	½ cup chopped cilantro
1 tablespoon soy sauce	

FOR THE MEATBALLS: Combine the ground pork, garlic powder, black pepper, salt, and soy sauce in a mixing bowl. Mix well with your hands and form into small balls, 1 tablespoon each.

FOR THE SOUP: Peel and quarter the cucumber lengthwise and cut in ¼-inch pieces.

In a medium pot, bring 4 cups water to a boil. Add meatballs one at a time and cook 5 minutes. Add cucumber and salt. Bring to a boil, add scallion and turn off the heat. Add cilantro before serving.

SERVES 4

Duck Soup

GANG PIT

Bones from page 115	2 tablespoons fish sauce
4 slices dried or fresh kalanga	1 medium tomato, quartered and
1 stalk fresh lemongrass, cut into	sliced
3-inch pieces or ¼ cup dried	2 stalks scallions, chopped
3 kaffir lime leaves	½ cup chopped cilantro
1 teaspoon salt	

In a large pot add 8 cups water and bring to a boil. Add duck bones, bring to a boil, turn the heat to medium, cover and simmer 45 minutes. Discard the bones, strain the broth, and drain fat. Transfer to a clean medium pot. Add kalanga, lemongrass, kaffir lime leaves and salt. Bring to a boil, cover, and simmer 20 minutes or longer, until the broth amounts to 5 cups. Turn the heat to high and bring it to a full boil. Add fish sauce, tomato, and scallion. Mix well and turn off the heat. Add cilantro before serving.

Serve hot with Duck Lob (page 116).

SERVES 2 TO 4

Fish and Chinese Radish Soup

GANG PA HORE PUCK GOT

1 pound mud fish fillet, cut 1 inch widthwise	1 tablespoon red curry paste
2 cups cubed Chinese white radish	4 tablespoons tamarind juice
1 teaspoon salt	2 stalks scallions, chopped
2 tablespoons fish sauce	

In a medium pot, bring 6 cups water to a boil on high heat. Add fish, radish, salt, fish sauce, curry paste, and tamarind juice, and cook 5 minutes. Add scallions, stir well, and turn off the heat.

Serve as a soup or with rice as a meal.

SERVES 4 TO 6

Fish Soup

GANG SOME PA

1 stalk fresh lemongrass, cut in 2-inch pieces across the grain or 2 tablespoons dried	1 teaspoon salt
	2 tablespoons fish sauce
	2 tablespoons lime or tamarind juice
4 slices dried or fresh kalanga	1 large firm ripe tomato, cut in ½-inch cubes
4 kaffir lime leaves	
1 pound stripe bass fish fillet, cut 1 inch widthwise	2 stalks scallions, chopped

In a medium pot, add 8 cups water, lemongrass, kalanga, and kaffir lime leaves. Bring to a boil on high heat. Cover and simmer 30 minutes. The broth will reduce to 6 cups.

Turn the heat on high to a boil. Add fish, salt, and fish sauce (if using tamarind juice instead of lime, add it now), and cook 3 minutes. Add tomato and scallion, stir well, and turn off the heat. Add lime juice before serving.

Serve with rice and Raw Fish Lob (page 118).

SERVES 2 TO 4

Mushroom Soup

TOME SOUP HIT

1 head garlic	5 ounces fresh button mushrooms, quartered
4 shallots or 1 medium onion, sliced	5 ounces fresh oyster mushrooms
1½ inches fresh ginger, sliced in 6 pieces across the grain	1 package (3.5 ounces) fresh shiitake mushrooms
1 stalk fresh lemongrass, cut in 2-inch pieces across the grain or 2 tablespoons dried	1 package (3.5 ounces) enoki mushrooms
1 large hot pepper or ¼ bell pepper for a non-spicy dish	1 teaspoon salt
	2 tablespoons fish sauce (optional)
	2 stalks scallions, chopped
3 kaffir lime leaves (optional)	1 cup chopped cilantro

Preheat oven on broil.

In a roasting pan place garlic, shallots, ginger, lemongrass, and pepper. Roast 8 minutes on each side and let cool.

Chop garlic, shallots, and pepper and set aside.

In a medium pot, bring 5 cups water to a boil. Add ginger, lemongrass, and kaffir lime leaves. Cover and simmer 30 minutes. Turn the heat high and add mushrooms, garlic, shallots, pepper, salt, and fish sauce. Bring to a boil and cook 5 minutes. Add scallions, stir well, and turn off the heat. Add cilantro before serving.

SERVES 6

Rice Noodle Soup

KOW PIAK SEN

1 pound boneless chicken breast	1 teaspoon crushed hot pepper
2 teaspoons salt	(optional)
1 pound fresh rice noodles	1 tablespoon soy sauce
1 head garlic	1 tablespoon fish sauce
1 inch fresh ginger, peeled and	2 stalks scallions, chopped
sliced across the grain	1 cup chopped cilantro
3 tablespoons olive oil	1 teaspoon ground black pepper

In a large pot, bring 8 cups water to a boil. Add chicken and salt and bring to a boil. Turn the heat to medium, cover, and cook 15 minutes. Take the chicken out and let it cool. Turn the heat to high and add the noodles, stir well, and bring to a boil. Turn the heat to medium and cook 10 minutes.

While the noodles are cooking, combine garlic and ginger in a mini chopper and chop 10 seconds. Heat a small saucepan with oil on high heat. Add garlic and ginger and stir constantly until light brown, 3 minutes. Let cool for a minute. Add hot pepper, stir well, and set aside.

The chicken should be cool by now. Shred it and add to the soup. Add soy sauce, fish sauce, garlic, ginger, and hot pepper mixture and bring to a boil. Add scallions, stir well, and turn off the heat.

Serve in large soup bowls. Add cilantro and black pepper to each bowl before serving.

SERVES 4

Rice Soup

KOW PIAK

1 pound boneless chicken breast	1 teaspoon crushed hot pepper
1 cup rice, rinsed well and drained	(optional)
2 teaspoons salt	1 tablespoon soy sauce
1 head garlic	1 tablespoon fish sauce
1 inch fresh ginger, peeled and	2 stalks scallions, chopped
sliced across the grain	1 cup chopped cilantro
3 tablespoons olive oil	Black pepper to taste

In a large pot, bring 8 cups water to a boil. Add chicken, rice, and salt, stir well, and cook on medium heat 15 minutes. Take the chicken out and let cool. Continue cooking the rice another 15 minutes, stirring occasionally.

While the rice is cooking, combine the garlic and ginger in a mini chopper. Chop 10 seconds. Heat a small saucepan with oil on high heat. Add garlic and ginger and stir constantly until light brown, 3 minutes. Turn off the heat and let cool for a minute. Add hot pepper, stir well, and set aside.

The chicken should be cool by now. Shred it and add to the soup. Add soy sauce, fish sauce, garlic, ginger, and hot pepper mixture and bring to a boil. Add scallions, stir well, and turn off the heat.

Serve in large soup bowls. Add cilantro and black pepper to each bowl before serving.

SERVES 4

Seafood Soup

TOME YUM TALAY

2 stalks fresh lemongrass, cut in
   2-inch pieces across the grain or
   2 tablespoons dried
4 slices fresh or dried kalanga
   (optional)
4 kaffir lime leaves (optional)
1 pound clams
1 pound mussels
2 teaspoons salt
4 tablespoons fish sauce

¼ pound squid, cut into bite-size
   pieces
¼ pound scallops
¼ pound shrimp, peeled and
   cleaned
2 tablespoons chili and garlic paste
3 stalks scallions, chopped
1 cup chopped cilantro
4 tablespoons lime juice

In a large pot, add 10 cups water, lemongrass, kalanga, and kaffir lime leaves. Bring to a boil, cover, and simmer 30 minutes. It will reduce to 8 cups.

Turn the heat to high and add clams, mussels, salt, and fish sauce. Stir well, bring to a boil, and cook 5 minutes. Add squid, scallops and shrimp. Stir well and return to a boil. Add chili paste and scallions, stir well, and turn off the heat. Add cilantro and lime juice before serving.

SERVES 10

Shrimp in Lemongrass Soup

TOME YUM GOUNG

Tofu has a lot of protein and no fat, so I try to add it to many dishes. It tastes great in this soup, so try it. You can sneak a little in any dish that you cook. Just cut it small so that no one minds.

1 stalk fresh lemongrass, cut in 2-inch pieces across the grain or 2 tablespoons dried	1 pound shrimp, peeled and cleaned
2 slices fresh or dried kalanga (optional)	1 can (15 ounces) straw mushrooms, drained or ¼ pound fresh button mushrooms, sliced
2 kaffir lime leaves (optional)	1 tablespoon chili and garlic paste
1 teaspoon salt	1 stalk scallion, chopped
2 tablespoons fish sauce	½ cup chopped cilantro
½ package (7.5 ounces) tofu, cut in ½-inch cubes	2 tablespoons lime juice

In a medium pot, add 8 cups water, lemongrass, kalanga, and kaffir lime leaves. Bring to a boil, cover, and simmer 30 minutes. It will reduce to 5 cups.

Turn the heat to high and add tofu, salt, and fish sauce. Stir well and bring to a boil. Add shrimp and mushrooms. Stir well and return to a boil. Add chili paste and scallion.

Stir well and turn off the heat. Add cilantro and lime juice before serving.

SERVES 6

Tofu Soup

GANG TAO HOU

Tofu soup is very light and tasty if you make it my way. This soup is great for children.

MEATBALLS:	SOUP:
1 pound ground pork or turkey	1 package (1.7 ounces) cellophane
½ teaspoon salt	noodles
½ teaspoon ground black pepper	1 package (15 ounces) tofu, cut in
1½ tablespoons soy sauce	½-inch cubes
2 teaspoons garlic powder	2 teaspoons salt
	1 tablespoon soy sauce
	2 stalks scallions, chopped
	½ cup chopped cilantro
	½ teaspoon ground white pepper

FOR THE MEATBALLS: Combine ground pork, salt, black pepper, soy sauce, and garlic powder in a large mixing bowl. Mix well with your hands (use gloves if desired) and form into balls of 2 tablespoons each.

FOR THE SOUP: Soak cellophane noodles in warm water for 15 minute, drain, and cut in 4-inch-long pieces.

In a medium pot, bring 8 cups water to a boil. Drop the meatballs in the water one at a time and return to a boil. Add tofu, salt, and soy sauce. Stir well and cook 5 minutes.

Add cellophane noodles and stir well. Bring to a boil, add scallions and turn off the heat. Let it set 5 minutes. Add cilantro and white pepper before serving.

SERVES 8

Vegetable Rib Soup

GANG PUCK

1 pound pork rib, cut in bite-size pieces	1 medium zucchini, cut in bite-size pieces
2 teaspoons salt	2 tablespoons fish sauce (optional)
¼ pound green beans, cut in half	¼ pound napa cabbage, cut in bite-size pieces
¼ pound sugar snap peas, stemmed	
¼ pound broccoli, cut in bite-size pieces	

In a large pot, bring 8 cups water to a boil. Add pork ribs and salt. Stir well and bring to a boil. Cover and simmer for 45 minutes. Let cool and drain fat.

Transfer to a clean pot and return to a boil on high heat. Add green beans and return to a boil. Cover and cook 3 minutes. Add peas, broccoli, zucchini, and fish sauce. Stir well, return to a boil and cook 2 minutes. Add napa cabbage, stir well, and turn off the heat.

Serve as a soup or with hot sauce and rice for light meal.

SERVES 4

Watercress Soup

GANG PUCK NUM

Here is another dish in which you can add tofu. It tastes very good.

2 or 3 pounds pork neck bones or chicken bones	½ package (7.5 ounces) tofu, cut in ¼-inch cubes
1 bunch watercress	1 stalk scallion, chopped
2 teaspoons salt	

In a medium pot add 8 cups water and bring to a boil on high heat. Add bones and return to a boil. Cover and simmer 45 minutes. It will reduce to 6 cups.

While the bones are simmering, soak watercress in cold water 10 minutes.

Wash well, drain, and cut in ½-inch pieces.

Discard the bones and let the broth cool. Strain and drain fat. Transfer the broth to a clean pot and bring to a boil. Add salt and tofu. Stir well and cook 5 minutes.

Add watercress, stir well, and bring to a boil. Add scallion, stir well, and turn off the heat.

SERVES 6

Winter Melon Soup

GANG MOCK TONE

2 or 3 pounds pork neck bones or chicken bones	1 pound winter melon, cut into ¼-inch cubes
2 teaspoons salt	2 stalks scallions, chopped

In a medium pot add 8 cups water and bring to a boil. Add bones and return to a boil. Cover and simmer 45 minutes. The broth will reduce to 6 cups.

Discard the bones and let the broth cool. Strain and drain fat. Transfer to a clean pot and bring to a boil. Add salt and winter melon and cook 3 minutes. Add scallions, stir well, and turn off the heat.

SERVES 6

Salads and Sauces

Carrot Salad

TUM GARROT

There was no green papaya available on Long Island, New York, in 1980 when I first came to the United States. My sisters and I craved papaya salad. Someone told us to simply substitute carrots for papaya, which worked out great. We now enjoy this salad as much as papaya salad. Of course, we Laotian women like it extremely spicy.

½ pound carrots	5 cherry tomatoes, quartered
2 small red hot peppers (more or less as you desire)	1½ tablespoons fish sauce
1 clove garlic	1 tablespoon sugar
½ tablespoon shrimp paste (optional)	1 tablespoon lime juice

Peel and shred the carrots thin and long (a food processor or a food slicer works very well). Make 2 cups and place in a large mixing bowl.

Combine hot peppers, garlic, and shrimp paste in a mini chopper. Chop 10 seconds and transfer to the bowl with the carrots. Add tomatoes, fish sauce, sugar and lime juice. With both hands, using gloves if desired, mix and squeeze at the same time until all ingredients are well mixed and soft, about 10 times. Transfer to a serving plate and accompany with sliced green cabbage or green lettuce leaves.

Serve as an appetizer or side dish with grilled chicken or pork and sticky rice.

SERVES 2

Cucumber Salad

TUM MOCK TANG

1 pound Kirby cucumber	5 cherry tomatoes, half or quarter
2 small red hot peppers	2 tablespoons fish sauce
(more or less as you desire)	1½ tablespoons sugar
1 clove garlic	1½ tablespoons lime juice
½ tablespoon shrimp paste	
(optional)	

Peel and julienne the cucumber thin and long and place in a large mixing bowl.

Combine hot peppers, garlic, and shrimp paste in a mini chopper. Chop 10 seconds and transfer to the bowl with cucumber. Add tomatoes, fish sauce, sugar, and lime juice. With both hands, using gloves if desired, mix lightly until all ingredients are well mixed, about 5 times.

Serve as an appetizer or side dish with grilled chicken and rice.

SERVES 2

Green Mango Salad

YUM MOCK MUANG

When mango is in season, Laotian women get together and enjoy this dish as an afternoon snack.

1 large green mango	½ teaspoon salt
2 cloves garlic, minced	2 tablespoons fish sauce
2 red chili peppers, minced (optional)	2 shallots, thinly sliced
2 tablespoons sugar	

Peel and julienne the mango and place in a large mixing bowl. Add garlic, pepper, sugar, salt, and fish sauce. With both hands, using gloves if desired, mix and squeeze at the same time until all ingredients are soft and well mixed, about 10 times. Add shallots and mix well.

Serve as an appetizer or afternoon snack.

SERVES 2

Grilled Portabella Salad

YUM PING HIT

6 ounces portabella mushroom	1 stalk scallion, chopped
½ teaspoon salt	½ cup chopped cilantro
1½ tablespoons fish sauce (optional)	1 cup mesclun
2 tablespoons lime juice	

Grill portabella without rubbing oil on, 4 minutes on each side. Let cool 5 minutes.

Cut in half and slice ¼ inch thick. Place in a large mixing bowl. Add salt, fish sauce, and lime juice. Mix well with a spoon. Add scallion and cilantro and mix lightly.

Spread mesclun on a serving plate. Transfer the mixture to the center.

SERVES 4

Papaya Salad

TUM MOCK HOUNG

Laotian women enjoy this dish during summer afternoon get-togethers, always making extremely spicy. I prepare this dish almost every time my family gets together and it is also the dish I choose when I need to diet.

½ pound green papaya	5 cherry tomatoes, quartered
2 small red hot peppers (more or less as you desire)	1½ tablespoons fish sauce
1 clove garlic	1 tablespoon sugar
½ tablespoon shrimp paste (optional)	1 tablespoon lime juice

Peel and shred the papaya thin and long (a food processor or food slicer works very well) and place in a large mixing bowl.

Combine hot peppers, garlic, and shrimp paste in a mini chopper and chop 5 seconds. Transfer to the bowl with the papaya. Add tomatoes, fish sauce, sugar, and lime juice.

With both hands, using gloves if desired, mix and squeeze at the same time until all ingredients are well mixed and soft, about 10 times. Transfer to serving plate and accompany with sliced green cabbage or green leaves lettuce.

Serve as an appetizer or side dish with grilled chicken, steak, or pork and sticky rice.

SERVES 2

Penn's Salad

Mint, cilantro, and watercress are available in most supermarkets; add them to your salads. They taste great together and remind you of spring year-round.

SALAD	DRESSING
4 large eggs	4 egg yolks
2 cups mesclun	1/3 cup olive oil
1/2 cup cilantro leaves	6 cloves garlic, chopped
1/2 cup mint leaves	1 tablespoon salt
1/2 cup Chinese or regular	3 tablespoons sugar
celery leaves (optional)	2 tablespoons lime juice
1 cup watercress	
1 Kirby cucumber, peeled	1/4 cup roasted peanuts
and sliced	
10 sherry tomatoes, halved	

FOR THE SALAD: Boil the eggs for 30 minutes, transfer to cold water and let stand for 15 minutes. Peel the eggs and cut them in half, reserving the yolks to make the dressing. Slice the egg whites and set aside.

Mix mesclun, cilantro, mint, celery, and watercress in large bowl. Transfer to serving plates and top with cucumber, tomatoes, and egg whites.

FOR THE DRESSING: Place the yolks in a medium powl, and mash with a whisk.

Heat a small saucepan with oil on medium heat. Add garlic and stir constantly until light brown, 2 minutes. Add to the egg yolks and whisk well. Add salt, sugar, and lime juice and whisk until creamy.

Drizzle on top of salad and sprinkle with chopped peanuts.

SERVES 4

Spring Salad

YUM SA LUD

2 cups chopped red or green lettuce leaves	1 small cucumber, peeled and sliced
½ cup cilantro leaves	1 small ripe tomato, halved and sliced
½ cup mint leaves	
1 cup watercress	

Mix lettuce, cilantro, mint, and watercress in a large bowl. Transfer to serving plates and top with cucumber and tomato. Add Peanut Dressing or Satay Sauce (page 62).

SERVES 4

Shrimp Salad

YUM GOUNG

3 tablespoons olive oil	2 tablespoons lime juice
4 cloves garlic, chopped	1 tablespoon fresh lemongrass,
1 pound shrimp, peeled and	thinly sliced across the grain
cleaned	1 small white onion, sliced
½ teaspoon dried hot pepper	1 stalk scallion, chopped
(optional)	½ cup chopped cilantro
½ teaspoon salt	1 cup mesclun
1½ tablespoons fish sauce	

Heat a medium wok or pan with oil on high heat. Add garlic and stir constantly until light brown, 2 minutes. Add shrimp and stir constantly for 3 minutes. Transfer to a large mixing bowl and let cool 5 minutes.

Add hot pepper, salt, fish sauce, lime juice, lemongrass, and onion. Mix well with a spoon. Add scallion and cilantro and mix lightly. Spread mesclun on a serving plate and transfer the mixture on top.

SERVES 2

Chopped Fresh Pepper Sauce

JAIL SOY

1 teaspoon chopped fresh chili pepper	2 tablespoons lime juice
1 teaspoon chopped scallion	2 tablespoons fish sauce
1 teaspoon chopped cilantro	

Combine all ingredients in small sauce bowl and mix well.

Serve with steak, grilled chicken, grilled fish, or egg dishes.

SERVES 4

Dried Pepper and Fish Sauce

JAIL PONG NUM PA

Mix 1 teaspoon crushed dried pepper and 1 tablespoon fish sauce.

SERVES 2

Dried Pepper and Soy Sauce

JAIL PONG SEE EW

Mix 1 teaspoon crushed dried pepper and 1 tablespoon soy sauce.

SERVES 2

Fresh Pepper and Fish Sauce

JAIL SOY NUM PA

Mix 2 teaspoon chopped chili pepper and 1 tablespoon fish sauce.

SERVES 2

Fresh Pepper and Soy Sauce

JAIL SOY SEE EW

Mix 2 teaspoons chopped fresh chili pepper with 1 tablespoon soy sauce.

SERVES 2

Ginger Sauce

JAIL KING

Ginger is very fibrous so it must be cut across the grain before chopping.
Ginger sauce goes very well with roasted or barbecued chicken.

2 inches fresh ginger, peeled and sliced across the grain	1 tablespoon fish sauce
	1 tablespoon soy sauce
2 cloves garlic	1 tablespoon sugar
1 red chili pepper (optional)	1 tablespoon lime juice

Combine all ingredients and 3 tablespoons water in a blender and blend 10 seconds.

It should taste spicy, sweet, and sour, and tastes better if refrigerated overnight.

It lasts about 3 weeks refrigerated in an airtight container.

SERVES 4

Green Pepper Sauce

JAIL MOCK PIT DIP

3 large green hot peppers	1½ tablespoons fish sauce
4 cloves garlic	2 tablespoons chopped cilantro

Poke a couple of holes in the peppers and grill on high heat until blistered, 5 minutes each side.

Thread a bamboo stick through the garlic and grill on high heat until blistered, 8 minutes on each side.

Cut each pepper in 4 pieces and transfer to a mini chopper. Add garlic and fish sauce, chop 5 seconds. Add cilantro, turn it on and off immediately. Transfer to small sauce bowl and serve with sticky rice and grilled pork, beef, chicken, or fish. This sauce also goes well with vegetable soup.

SERVES 2

Peanut Sauce

JAIL TORE DIN

This peanut sauce is served as a dipping sauce with fresh and fried spring rolls, crepes, vegetable wraps or anything you like. Save the unused portion in an airtight container and freeze. It will last for a couple of months. People who like spicy dishes should add dried crushed hot pepper to their own bowl.

½ cup sugar	1½ tablespoons lime juice
1 teaspoon salt	1 chili pepper or dried crushed hot
1 tablespoon fish sauce	pepper (optional)
1 clove garlic	¼ cup chopped roasted peanuts
¼ cup peanut butter	

In a medium pot, caramelize the sugar on medium heat until golden brown. For safety, bring the hot pot of caramelized sugar to the sink, step away, and then add 1 cup hot water. It will steam up, so be very careful. If you are not experienced, wait for a couple of minutes for it to cool, then add the hot water.

Bring the pot back to the stove and boil until the sugar dissolves. Cover with a lid for faster results. Let cool 30 minutes.

Transfer to a blender and add salt, fish sauce, garlic, peanut butter, lime juice, and pepper. Blend 30 seconds.

For extra flavor, place roasted peanuts in a frying pan on high heat. Shake and stir constantly 3 minutes. Let cool 15 minutes. Chop in a mini chopper 5 seconds and set aside. You can also skip this step and chop the roasted peanuts from the jar.

Serve in individual sauce bowls and garnish with the roasted peanuts.

SERVES 4

Plum Sauce

JAIL PLUM

Plum sauce is served with roasted duck or fried spring rolls (Do not add ginger if serving with fried spring rolls.)

1 cup honey	2 teaspoons salt
2 plums, peeled and sliced	2 tablespoons cornstarch
¼ cup soy sauce	½ cup julienned fresh ginger

In a medium saucepan add honey and bring to a boil on medium heat. Add plums and stir constantly 3 minutes. Add soy sauce and salt, stir well, and cook 2 minutes. Add ¾ cup water and simmer 5 minutes. Mix cornstarch with ⅓ cup water and slowly add to the sauce, stirring constantly for a minute. Add ginger, mix well, and turn off the heat.

Let it set 2 minutes allowing the sauce to thicken. Pour on roasted duck or serve with fried spring rolls at room temperature.

SERVES 4

Roasted Green Pepper and Fish Sauce

JAIL JEEK

Peppers can be roasted on a gas or electric stove, as well as on a grill.

1 large green hot pepper	1 tablespoon fish sauce or soy sauce

Hold the pepper with tongs over a medium frame gas or electric and turn constantly until blistered, 2 minutes. Place the pepper on cutting board and julienne it. Transfer to a small sauce bowl, add fish sauce, mix well, and serve.

SERVES 2

Satay Sauce

NUM SATAY

This sauce is used as Satay Sauce and Peanut Dressing for Spring Salad.

1 tablespoon olive oil	2 teaspoons salt
1 tablespoon yellow curry powder	1 tablespoon fish sauce (optional)
1 can (13.5 ounces) coconut milk	½ cup peanut butter
¼ cup sugar	2 tablespoons tamarind or lime juice

Heat a medium wok or frying pan with oil on medium heat. Add curry and stir for 3 seconds. Add coconut milk and bring to a boil. Add sugar, salt, fish sauce, peanut butter, and tamarind juice. Turn the heat to low and stir constantly until creamy, 5 minutes.

Keep it warm to serve with Satay (page 17) or let it cool to room temperature and serve as a salad dressing with Spring Salad (page 54).

SERVES 6

Seafood Sauce

JAIL SOME TALAY

This sauce is a much better dipping sauce for lobster than plain melted butter.

2 red hot chili peppers or 1 tablespoon chopped red bell pepper for a non-spicy dish 2 cloves garlic	1 tablespoons sugar 1 teaspoon salt 3 tablespoons lime juice 2 tablespoons fish sauce

In a blender, add peppers, garlic, sugar, salt, lime juice, fish sauce, and $\frac{1}{2}$ cup water. Blend 15 seconds. Transfer to a small sauce bowl and serve as a dipping sauce with lobster or any steamed seafood.

SERVES 2

Sweet and Sour Sauce

JAIL SOME

Serve as a side sauce with chicken, steak, fish, vegetables, rice, or anything you desire. This dish is perfect for someone who likes very spicy food.

10 red hot chili peppers	1 teaspoon salt
2 cloves garlic	1 tablespoon lime juice
2 tablespoons sugar	2 tablespoons fish sauce

In a blender, add peppers, garlic, sugar, salt, lime juice, fish sauce, and ¼ cup water. Blend 15 seconds. This tastes best after refrigerating overnight in an airtight container.

SERVES 2

Tomato Sauce

JAIL MOCK LENT

This is a great sauce to serve with rice and steamed vegetables for vegetarians. I make this sauce and eat it with steamed vegetables when I need to loose a few pounds.

1 head garlic	2 teaspoons salt
6 shallots or 1 medium onion, sliced	2 tablespoons fish sauce (optional)
2 large red hot peppers (optional)	1 tablespoon sugar
1 red bell pepper	$\frac{1}{2}$ cup chopped cilantro
2 large tomatoes, halved	

Preheat oven on broil.

On a baking pan, place garlic, shallots, hot peppers, red pepper and tomatoes (do not oil them). Broil 10 minutes on each side. Turn off the heat and let them sit in the oven 15 minutes.

In a food processor, add garlic, shallots, hot peppers and red pepper. Chop 10 seconds. Add tomatoes, salt, fish sauce and sugar. Chop another 5 seconds.

It should be a little chunky. Add cilantro and turn on and off immediately.

Serve as a side sauce with roasted chicken, steamed vegetables, and rice.

SERVES 4

Rice and Noodles

Chicken Fried Rice

KORE KAO

4 tablespoons oil	½ teaspoon ground black pepper
1 head garlic, chopped	1 medium white onion, chopped
½ pound boneless chicken, sliced in bite-size pieces, or shrimp, peeled and cleaned	2 large eggs, lightly beaten
	3 cups cooked rice
	2 stalks scallions, chopped
1 teaspoon salt	½ cup chopped cilantro
3 tablespoons soy sauce	

Heat a wok or frying pan with oil on high heat. Add garlic and stir constantly until light brown, 2 minutes. Add chicken and stir constantly 3 minutes. Add salt, soy sauce, black pepper, and onion and stir well for another 2 minutes.

Turn the heat to medium, add the eggs and wait 30 seconds before stirring lightly. Add the rice and stir constantly for 5 minutes. Add scallions, stir well, and turn off the heat. Add cilantro, stir lightly, and transfer to a serving plate.

SERVES 2

Pineapple Fried Rice

KORE KAO MOCK NUT

4 tablespoons olive oil	½ fresh pineapple, peeled and
1 head garlic, chopped	cubed
½ pound shrimp, peeled and	1 medium white onion, chopped
cleaned	2 cups cooked rice
1 teaspoon salt	2 stalks scallions, chopped
3 tablespoons soy sauce	½ cup chopped cilantro
½ teaspoon ground white pepper	

Heat a wok or frying pan with oil on high heat. Add garlic and stir until light brown, 2 minutes. Add shrimp and stir constantly for 1 minute. Add salt, soy sauce, and pepper and stir constantly another 30 seconds. Add pineapple and onion and stir constantly 2 minutes. Add rice and stir constantly for 5 minutes.

Add scallions, stir well, and turn off the heat. Add cilantro, stir lightly, and transfer to a serving plate.

SERVES 2

Rice in Chicken Broth

KAO MUN GICE

Serve with roasted duck, plum sauce, and sautéed Chinese broccoli.

2 or 3 pounds chicken bones	2 cups rice, rinsed and drained well
3 tablespoons olive oil	1 teaspoon salt
1 head garlic, chopped	3 tablespoons soy sauce
1 large onion, chopped	

In a large pot, bring 6 cups water to a boil on high heat. Add chicken bones, bring to a boil. Cover and simmer for 45 minutes. The broth will reduce to 3 cups.

Discard the bones and keep the broth hot.

Heat a large nonstick pot with oil on high heat. Add garlic and onion and stir constantly for 5 minutes until light brown. Add rice and stir constantly until light brown, 5 minutes. Add broth, salt, and soy sauce. Stir well and bring to a boil.

Turn the heat to low, cover, and simmer 15 minutes. Turn off the heat and let it sit 15 minutes before serving.

SERVES 6

Rice in Duck Broth

KAO MUN PIT

Use the duck bones and unwanted items from Roasted Duck (page 102).

2 pounds duck bones and innards	2 cups rice, rinsed and drained well
3 tablespoons olive oil	1 teaspoon salt
1 head garlic, chopped	3 tablespoons soy sauce
1 large onion, chopped	

In a large pot, bring 6 cups water to a boil on high heat. Add duck bones and return to a boil. Cover and simmer 45 minutes. The broth will reduce to 3 cups. Discard the bones and innards and keep the broth hot.

Heat a large pot with oil on high heat. Add garlic and onion and stir constantly until light brown, 5 minutes. Add rice and stir constantly until light brown, 5 minutes. Add broth, salt, and soy sauce. Stir well and bring to a boil. Turn the heat to low, cover, and simmer 15 minutes. Turn off the heat and let it sit 15 minutes before serving.

Serve with roasted chicken, ginger sauce, and sautéed Chinese broccoli.

SERVES 6

Soy Sauce Fried Rice

KORE KAO SEE EW

3 cups cooked rice	2 tablespoons soy sauce
3 tablespoons black soy sauce	1 teaspoon salt
4 tablespoons olive oil	1 medium white onion, chopped
2 large eggs, lightly beaten	½ teaspoon ground black pepper
1 head garlic, chopped	2 stalks scallions chopped
½ pound ground pork or turkey	½ cup chopped cilantro

Crumble the rice and mix with the thick soy sauce. Make sure that all the rice is coated and set aside.

Heat a wok or frying pan with 1 tablespoon oil on medium heat. Add the eggs and wait 1 minute, then flip them to cook the other side for another minute. Transfer to a plate, let cool and chop. Add the remaining 3 tablespoons oil to the same wok and heat on high heat.

Add garlic and stir constantly until light brown, 2 minutes. Add pork and stir constantly until the juice from the meat dries, 5 minutes. Add thin soy sauce, salt, onion, pepper, and egg. Stir well 30 seconds. Add rice and stir constantly for 5 minutes. Add scallions, stir well, and turn off the heat. Add cilantro, stir lightly, and transfer to a serving plate.

SERVES 2

Sticky Rice or Sweet Rice

KAO NEAL

Before making anything at all, sticky rice must be made. Since Laotians eat rice with almost every meal, the rice is presoaked the night before, cooked first thing in the morning, and should suffice for breakfast and lunch. By noon, another bowl should be soaked for dinner. At dinner, rice must be hot for the most important meal of the day.

In Laos every night before I went to bed, my mother told me "Soak the rice." Why couldn't I just cook it? I never got the explanation. One day I forgot to soak the rice, so I wet the rice and steamed it like always. My mother soon noticed that the rice wasn't cooking. I haven't forgotten to soak the rice since! Perhaps I didn't really forget, maybe it was just an experiment. My mother never knew.

1 cup sticky rice per serving

Soak the rice in warm water at least 2 hours. Fill the pot with water up to 3 inches from the bottom and place on the stove over high heat (make sure that the rice will not touch the water when the steamer basket is inserted).

Strain the rice in the steamer basket, rinse well, drain out the excess water, and place the basket on the steamer pot. Steam with a cover on high heat for 20 minutes, until the rice is cooked. Take the basket off the pot, wet a wooden spoon and stir the rice for a minute to cool then transfer to a bamboo rice keeper.

HOW TO REHEAT THE RICE: Fill the pot with water up to 3 inches from bottom and place it on the stove over high heat. Wet the steamer basket, break the rice in small pieces, replace it in the basket, and steam until the rice is soft, about 10 minutes. When the rice is reheated, it cooks faster and tastes softer.

NOTE: The rice stays good at room temperature for a couple of days, but must be reheated within 24 hours or it will dry up. Place the cool leftover rice in a plastic bag and refrigerate until ready to reheat.

HOW TO POP THE RICE: Cooked dried rice can be fried, which will make it pop like rice cakes. The rice must be completely dried before frying. Dry the leftover cooked rice in the sun until completely dried, 3 to 4 days. Fill a medium pot with 3 inches of oil from the bottom. Turn the heat on high. Wait until the oil gets very hot. Add dried rice, which will pop in a second. Stir constantly until golden brown. Scoop the rice out onto a large bowl with layers of paper towels to absorbs the access oil. Sprinkle with salt and eat it as a snack.

Vegetable Fried Rice

KORE KAO PUCK

Use vegetables that do not contain a lot of water to prevent the rice from being too moist.

4 tablespoons olive oil	1 cup chopped green cabbage
1 head garlic, chopped	1 medium white onion, chopped
½ cup chopped carrots	4 tablespoons soy sauce
½ cup frozen peas, thawed	1 teaspoon black pepper
½ cup green beans, cut ½ inch long	2 cups cooked rice
	2 stalks scallions, chopped
1 cup cubed marinated or regular tofu	½ cup chopped cilantro

Heat a wok or frying pan with oil on high heat. Add garlic and stir constantly until lightly brown, 2 minutes. Add carrots, peas, green beans, and tofu. Stir constantly for 5 minutes to cook and evaporate all water from the vegetables. Add cabbage, onion, soy sauce, and pepper and stir constantly another 30 seconds.

Turn the heat down to medium, add rice and stir constantly 5 minutes. Add scallions, stir well and turn off the heat. Add cilantro, stir lightly and transfer to a serving plate.

SERVES 2

Cellophane Noodles
with Chicken

YUM SEN RORN

2 packages (1.7 ounces each) cellophane noodles	1 teaspoon hot pepper (optional)
½ pound boneless chicken breast	2 tablespoons lime juice
1 teaspoon salt	1 stalk scallion, chopped
2 tablespoons fish sauce	½ cup chopped cilantro
	1 cup bean sprouts

Soak the noodles in warm water for 10 minutes. Drain and cut 4-inch-long pieces.

In a medium pot, bring 3 cups water to a boil on high heat. Add chicken and salt. Cook 10 minutes. Take out the chicken and let cool.

While the chicken is cooling, continue boiling the broth. Add the noodles, stir well, pour in a strainer, and immediately transfer to a large mixing bowl (do not let out all the excess water). Let cool 5 minutes.

While the noodles are cooling, shred the chicken and add it to the noodles. Add fish sauce, hot peppers and lime juice and mix well with both hands. Add scallion and mix well. Add the cilantro and mix lightly. Transfer to a serving plate, sprinkle with bean sprouts and serve at room temperature.

SERVES 2

Crispy Egg Noodles with Broccoli Gravy

MEE GRARB LOT NA

NOODLES:	3 tablespoons soy sauce
2 cups vegetable oil	1 tablespoon sugar
8 ounces egg noodles	½ teaspoon ground black pepper
	½ pound lean beef
GRAVY:	2 tablespoons cornstarch
2 tablespoons olive oil	1 stalk scallion, chopped
6 cloves garlic, chopped	½ cup chopped cilantro
3 cups chopped Chinese or regular broccoli	

FOR THE NOODLES: Heat a frying pan with vegetable oil on high heat. Add the noodles and fry until light brown, about a minute. Turn over to fry the other side another minute. Place on paper towels to absorb oil and keep warm.

FOR THE GRAVY: Heat the olive oil in a nonstick wok or pan on high heat. Add garlic, and stir constantly until lightly brown, 2 minutes. Add broccoli, soy sauce, sugar, and black pepper. Stir constantly 3 minutes. Add beef and continue stirring constantly another 2 minutes (the beef should be cooked until medium). Mix the starch with ½ cup water, stir into the broccoli, and cook another minute. Add scallion, stir well, and turn off the heat. Add cilantro and stir lightly.

Place the noodles on 2 serving plates. Pour gravy over the noodles and serve hot.

SERVES 2

Flat Rice Noodles in Clear Broth

PHER

This is a one dish per person meal. My family gets together just to have this dish. The broth is kept hot and hungry guests can serve themselves a bowl. This soup must be served immediately after making. You can make either all four bowls at once or one at a time.

8 ounces flat rice noodles	¼ cup olive oil
1 large onion, halved	2 tablespoons fish sauce
1 head garlic	4 tablespoons soy sauce
1 inch ginger, halved lengthwise	2 tablespoons sugar
3 pounds beef neck bones	1 cup chopped scallion
1 tablespoon salt	Ground black pepper to taste
1 pound lean beef, thinly sliced in	Hot pepper to taste (optional)
bite-size pieces	1 cup fresh bean sprouts
1 head garlic, chopped	1 cup chopped cilantro
6 shallots, chopped	1 large lime, quartered

Soak the noodles in warm water 30 minutes.

Preheat the oven on broil.

Place onion, garlic, and ginger on a tray, and broil 10 minutes on each side.

In a large pot, bring 4 quarts water to a boil on high heat. Add bones, onion, garlic, ginger, and salt and return to a boil. Turn the heat to low, cover and simmer 45 minutes (it will reduce to 8 cups). Discard the bones and strain, keeping only the broth. Keep it boiling.

Heat a small saucepan with oil on medium heat. Add garlic and shallots. Stir constantly until light brown.

Continued

Line up 4 large soup bowls.

In another medium pot add 6 cups water and bring to a boil. Add noodles, stir well, and strain. Divide equally among the soup bowls.

Put the beef in a strainer and dip the strainer into the boiling broth, mixing well for so the meat is cooked to your desire, rare to medium-well, 10 to 30 seconds. Let it drain and divide equally among the bowls. In each bowl add a fourth of the fish sauce, soy sauce, sugar, fried garlic and shallots, scallions, 1½ to 2 cups of broth, black pepper, hot pepper, sprouts, and cilantro. Give guests a lime quarter to squeeze into their own bowl.

SERVES 4

Flat Rice Noodles without Broth

PHER HANG

2 ounces flat rice noodles	1 tablespoon lime juice
2 cloves garlic, chopped	1 tablespoon chopped roasted
1 shallot, chopped	peanut
1½ teaspoons fish sauce	¼ teaspoon ground black pepper
¼ pound lean beef, thinly sliced in	½ stalk scallion, chopped
bite-size pieces	¼ cup chopped cilantro
1 tablespoon soy sauce	½ cup fresh bean sprouts
1½ teaspoons sugar	

Soak the noodles in warm water for 30 minutes.

Heat a small saucepan on medium high heat. Add garlic and shallots. Stir constantly until light brown, 5 minutes. Set aside.

In a medium pot, bring 2 cups water to a boil on high heat. Place beef in a strainer and dip in the boiling water. Stir well, remove from the heat, and strain, reserving the liquid. Transfer to a serving bowl.

Bring the liquid to a boil again. Add the noodles, stir well, strain and immediately transfer to the bowl of meat. Add fish sauce, soy sauce, sugar, lime juice, peanuts, garlic, shallot, black pepper, scallion, and cilantro. Mix well, top with bean sprouts and serve.

SERVES 1

Flat Rice Noodles, Peanuts and Marinated Tofu

KORE MEE/PUD THAI

If using lime juice, add it before serving.

8 ounces dried flat rice noodles	2 tablespoons tamarind juice
4 tablespoons olive oil	or lime juice
6 cloves garlic, chopped	1 cup cubed marinated tofu
¾ pound shrimp, peeled and	1 stalk scallion, chopped
cleaned, or chicken, sliced in	¼ cup crushed roasted peanuts
bite-size pieces	½ teaspoon crushed hot pepper
1 teaspoon salt	(optional)
2 tablespoons fish sauce	1 cup fresh bean sprouts
2 tablespoons soy sauce	½ cup chopped cilantro
2 tablespoons sugar	

Soak the noodles in warm water for 30 minutes.

Heat a wok with oil on high heat. Add garlic and stir constantly until light brown, 2 minutes. Add shrimp and stir constantly 2 minutes. Add salt, fish sauce, soy sauce, sugar, tamarind juice, and tofu. Stir constantly 2 minutes.

Add ½ cup water and bring to a boil. Add noodles, turn the heat to medium and mix well with tongs for 5 minutes. Add scallion, peanuts, hot pepper, (and bean sprouts if you like them cooked) and mix lightly. Add cilantro and mix lightly. Transfer to a serving plate and garnish with bean sprouts if you like them raw.

SERVES 4

Fresh Noodles with Broccoli

KORE PHER

2 tablespoons olive oil	1 tablespoon sugar
3 tablespoons sesame oil	½ teaspoon ground black pepper
6 cloves garlic, chopped	2 cups chopped Chinese or regular
½ pound lean beef, thinly sliced in	broccoli
bite-size pieces	12 ounces fresh rice noodles
3 tablespoons soy sauce	2 stalks scallions, chopped
3 tablespoons black soy sauce	½ cup chopped cilantro

Heat a wok or pan with oils on high heat. Add garlic and stir constantly until light brown, 2 minutes. Add beef and stir constantly for 30 seconds. Add thin soy sauce, black soy sauce, sugar, and black pepper. Stir constantly another 30 seconds to cook the beef medium done and take it out.

Cook the broth until thickened, 2 minutes. Add broccoli and stir constantly for 1 minute.

Turn the heat to medium, add noodles, and mix well 1 minute. Add the beef and scallions, mix well, and turn off the heat. Add cilantro, mix lightly, and transfer to a serving plate.

SERVES 2

Fresh Noodles with Broccoli Gravy

LOT NA

Fresh noodles are sometimes packed whole. Slice ½ inch wide before separating them.

NOODLES:
12 ounces fresh rice noodles
2 tablespoons olive oil
2 cloves garlic, chopped

GRAVY:
2 tablespoons olive oil
6 cloves garlic, chopped
2 cups chopped Chinese or regular broccoli

3 tablespoons soy sauce
1 tablespoon sugar
½ teaspoon ground black pepper
½ pound lean beef, sliced in bite-size pieces
2 tablespoons cornstarch
2 stalks scallions, chopped
½ cup chopped cilantro

FOR THE NOODLES: Separate the noodles by peeling each layer apart. Heat oil in a nonstick wok or pan on high heat. Add garlic and stir constantly until light brown, 2 minutes. Add noodles and stir well 2 minutes. Transfer to a serving plate and keep warm.

FOR THE GRAVY: Heat oil in a wok or pan on high heat. Add garlic and stir constantly until light brown, 2 minutes. Add broccoli, soy sauce, sugar and black pepper. Stir constantly for a minute. Add beef and continue stirring another minute (the beef should be medium). Mix cornstarch with ½ cup water, add to the beef, mix well and cook another minute. Add scallion, mix well, and turn off the heat. Pour over the noodles and sprinkle with cilantro.

SERVES 2

Rice Noodles with Clear Broth

KOA PUNE NUM JAIL

1 cup chopped lettuce of any kind	8 slices fresh or dried kalanga
½ cup chopped green cabbage	2 teaspoons salt
½ cup chopped purple cabbage	3 tablespoons fish sauce
2 stalks scallions, chopped	1 tablespoon sugar
1 cup bean sprouts	1 can (8 ounces) bamboo shoots,
½ cup mint leaves	sliced
½ cup cilantro leaves	9 ounces somen noodles
1 pound boneless pork or chicken	Dried hot pepper to taste (optional)

In a large bowl, mix the lettuce, green and purple cabbage, scallions, bean sprouts, mint, and cilantro. Set aside.

In a large pot, bring 3 quarts water to a boil on high heat. Add the pork, kalanga, and salt, and return to a boil. Cover and simmer 45 minutes (it will reduce to 8 cups).

While the pork is simmering, cook the noodles. Bring 2 quarts water to a boil in a medium pot. Add noodles, stir well, and return to a boil. Turn the heat to medium, stirring occasionally, and cook 5 minutes. Drain, rinse with cold water, and strain well 30 minutes.

Take the pork out of the broth and let it cool. Add fish sauce, sugar, bamboo shoots to the broth, cover, and keep on low heat. Slice the pork in bite-size pieces and add it back to the broth. Mix well and turn off the heat. Let it cool 15 minutes before serving.

Line up 4 large soup bowls. In each bowl, add a fourth of the greens, noodles, soup, and hot pepper. Serve warm and mix your own bowl with a spoon and chopsticks.

SERVES 4

Rice Noodles without Broth

KOA PUNE NUM PONG

I substitute ground turkey for pork for a low-fat dish.

1 cup chopped lettuce of any kind	½ pound ground pork or turkey
½ cup chopped green cabbage	½ teaspoon salt
½ cup chopped purple cabbage	4 tablespoons fish sauce
2 stalks scallions, chopped	4 tablespoons sugar
1 cup bean sprouts	4 tablespoons chopped roasted
½ cup mint leaves	peanuts
½ cup cilantro leaves	4 tablespoons lime juice
9 ounces somen noodles	Dried hot pepper to taste (optional)

In a large bowl, mix the lettuce, green and purple cabbage, scallions, bean sprouts, mint, and cilantro. Set aside.

Bring 8 cups water to a boil in a medium pot. Add noodles, stir well, and return to a boil. Turn the heat to medium, stir occasionally and cook 5 minutes. Drain, rinse with cold water and strain 30 minutes.

In a medium pan, add pork and salt. Cook on medium heat, without using oil. Stir constantly until dried (do not brown). Transfer to a large bowl lined with 3 pieces of paper towel to absorb the fat. Let cool 10 minutes. Transfer to a food processor and chop 30 seconds.

Line up 4 large soup bowls. In each bowl, add a fourth of the greens, noodles, pork, fish sauce, sugar, peanuts, lime juice, and hot pepper. Serve at room temperature. Mix your own bowl with a spoon and chopsticks.

SERVES 4

Red Curry Noodles

KOA PUNE NUM PIK

1 cup chopped lettuce of any kind	2 teaspoons salt
½ cup chopped green cabbage	½ pound boneless pork
½ cup chopped purple cabbage	2 cans (13.5 ounces) coconut milk
2 stalks scallions, chopped	3 tablespoons fish sauce (optional)
1 cup fresh bean sprouts	3 tablespoons sugar
½ cup mint leaves	2 tablespoons olive oil
½ cup cilantro leaves	2 tablespoons red curry paste
9 ounces somen noodles	½ pound ground pork or turkey
6 slices dried or fresh kalanga	1 can (8 ounces) sliced bamboo
4 kaffir lime leaves	

In a large bowl, mix the lettuce, cabbage, scallion, bean sprouts, mint, and cilantro. Set aside.

Bring 8 cups water to a boil in medium pot. Add noodles, stir well and return to a boil. Turn the heat to medium, stir occasionally, and cook 5 minutes. Rinse well with cold water, and strain for 30 minutes.

In a large pot, add 4 cups water, kalanga, kaffir lime leaves and salt. Bring to a boil and add the boneless pork. Cover and cook on medium heat 30 minutes. The broth will reduce to 2 cups. Take the pork out and let it cool. Add coconut milk, fish sauce, and sugar to the broth. Turn the heat high and bring to a boil.

Heat a wok or frying pan with oil on high heat. Add curry paste and mix well for 30 seconds. Add ground pork and stir constantly for 5 minutes. Transfer to the boiling broth.

The boneless pork should be cool by now. Cut the pork into strips and thinly slice in bite-size pieces. Add bamboo and pork to the broth, stir well, and bring to a boil. Turn the heat to low, cover, and simmer 15 minutes. Let cool 15 minutes before serving.

Line up 4 large soup bowls. In each bowl, add a fourth of the greens, noodles, and red curry soup. Serve warm and mix your own bowl with a spoon and chopsticks.

SERVES 4

Yellow Curry Noodles

KAO PUNE GALI

1 cup chopped lettuce of any kind	1½ pounds boneless chicken
½ cup chopped green cabbage	breast, cut in bite-size pieces
½ cup chopped purple cabbage	1 tablespoons salt
2 stalks scallions, chopped	3 tablespoons fish sauce (optional)
1 cup bean sprouts	2 tablespoons sugar
½ cup mint leaves	2 cans (13.5 ounces) coconut milk
½ cup cilantro leaves	1½ cups peeled and cubed pota-
9 ounces somen noodles	toes
2 tablespoons olive oil	1½ cup peeled and cubed sweet
2 tablespoons yellow curry powder	potatoes

In a large bowl, mix the lettuce, cabbage, scallions, bean sprouts, mint, and cilantro. Set aside.

Bring 2 quarts water to a boil in a medium pot. Add noodles, stir well, and bring to a boil. Turn the heat to medium, stir occasionally, and cook 5 minutes. Rinse with cold water, and strain 30 minutes.

Heat a large pot with oil on high heat. Add curry and stir 3 seconds. Add chicken and stir constantly 2 minutes. Add salt, fish sauce, and sugar and stir constantly 2 minutes, allowing the chicken to absorb the flavor. Add coconut milk and 2 cans of water (use the empty coconut milk can). Stir well and bring to a boil. Cover and simmer 20 minutes. Turn the heat to high and add potatoes and sweet potatoes. Stir well and bring to a boil. Turn the heat to medium, cover, and cook 8 minutes. Let it cool 15 minutes before serving.

Line up 4 large soup bowls. In each bowl add a fourth of the greens, noodles, and curry soup. Serve warm and mix your own bowl with a spoon and chopsticks.

SERVES 4

Entrées

Green Curry Beef

GANG KEO SEEN

2 tablespoons olive oil
1½ tablespoons green curry paste
1 pound lean beef, sliced in bite-size pieces
1 teaspoon salt
2 tablespoons fish sauce
1 tablespoon sugar (optional)
1 can (13.5 ounces) coconut milk
4 kaffir lime leaves (optional)

¼ pound green beans,
   cut 1 inch long
1 can (8 ounces) sliced bamboo,
   rinsed and drained
¼ pound eggplant, peeled and
   cubed
2 stalks scallion, cut 1 inch long
1 cup basil leaves

Heat a wok with oil on high heat. Add curry paste and mix well 1 minute. Add beef and stir constantly 2 minutes. Add salt, fish sauce, and sugar. Stir constantly another minute, allowing the beef to absorb the flavor. Add coconut milk and kaffir lime leaves and stir well. Cover and bring to a boil. Add green beans and bamboo and stir well. Cover and cook 3 minutes. Add eggplant, stirring well. Cover and cook another 3 minutes. Add scallions and basil. Stir well and transfer to a serving bowl.

Serve with rice, lettuce of any kind, and cucumber.

SERVES 2

Fresh Dill Chicken

KORE GICE PUCK SEE

When using lemongrass, remember to slice across the grain before blending, because lemongrass is very fibrous.

¼ cup sliced lemongrass	1 teaspoon salt
6 cloves garlic, chopped	2 tablespoons fish sauce (optional)
3 shallots or 1 small onion, sliced	½ red bell pepper, chopped
1 large hot pepper, sliced or ¼ bell pepper, sliced for a non-spicy dish	1 pound button mushrooms or brussels sprouts, quartered
2 tablespoons olive oil	2 stalks scallions, cut in 1-inch-long pieces
1 pound boneless chicken breast, sliced in bite-size pieces	1 cup chopped fresh dill

In a mini chopper add lemongrass and chop 10 seconds. Add garlic, shallots, and hot pepper. Chop another 10 seconds.

Heat a wok or pan with oil on high heat. Add garlic, shallots and pepper mixture.

Stir constantly until light brown, 3 minutes. Add chicken and stir constantly 1 minute. Add salt and fish sauce. Stir constantly another 30 seconds, allowing the chicken to absorb the flavor. Add red pepper and mushrooms. Cook 5 minutes, stirring occasionally. Add scallion and dill, stir well and transfer to a serving plate.

Serve with rice.

SERVES 2

Ginger Chicken

KORE GICE KING

When using ginger, remember to cut across the grain, because ginger is very fibrous.

3 tablespoons olive oil	1½ teaspoon oyster sauce (optional)
¼ cup julienned fresh ginger	1 small white onion, sliced
6 cloves garlic, chopped	2 cups sliced green, red and yellow
1 pound boneless chicken breast,	bell pepper
thinly sliced in bite-size pieces	1 large hot pepper, sliced (optional)
1 teaspoon salt	
1 tablespoon fish sauce (optional)	
1½ teaspoon soy sauce (optional)	

Heat a wok or pan with oil on high heat. Add ginger and stir constantly until light brown, 3 minutes. Add garlic and stir constantly until light brown, 2 minutes. Add chicken and stir constantly 1 minute. Add salt, fish sauce, soy sauce, and oyster sauce. Stir constantly 30 seconds, allowing the chicken to absorb the flavor. Add onion, bell pepper, and hot pepper. Stir constantly 3 minutes. The vegetables must remain crispy. Transfer to serving plate and serve with rice.

SERVES 2

Red Curry Chicken

GANG PIT GICE

2 tablespoons olive oil	¼ pound green beans,
1½ tablespoons red curry paste	cut into 1-inch pieces
1 pound boneless chicken breast,	1 can (8 ounces) sliced bamboo,
sliced in bite-size pieces	rinsed and drained
1 teaspoon salt	¼ pound eggplant, peeled and
2 tablespoons fish sauce	cubed
1 tablespoon sugar (optional)	2 stalks scallions, cut 1 inch long
1 can (13.5 ounces) coconut milk	1 cup basil leaves
4 kaffir lime leaves (optional)	

Heat a wok with oil on high heat. Add curry paste and mix well 1 minute. Add chicken and stir constantly 3 minutes. Add salt, fish sauce, and sugar. Stir constantly another 3 minutes, allowing the chicken to absorb the flavor. Add coconut milk and kaffir lime leaves. Stir well and bring to a boil. Add green beans and bamboo. Stir well, cover, and cook 3 minutes. Add eggplant and stir well. Cover and cook 3 minutes. Add scallions and basil. Stir well and transfer to a serving bowl.

Serve with rice, lettuce of any kind, and cucumber.

SERVES 2

SIMPLE LAOTIAN COOKING

Chicken with Spinach

ORM BORN

¼ cup sliced lemongrass, cut across the grain	4 kaffir lime leaves (optional)
6 cloves garlic	1 pound boneless chicken breast, cut in bite-size pieces
4 shallots or 1 small onion, sliced	1 teaspoon salt
1 large hot pepper, sliced or ¼ bell pepper, sliced for a non-spicy dish	2 tablespoons fish sauce (optional)
3 tablespoons olive oil	2 cans (13.5 ounces each) spinach, drained
4 slices fresh or dried kalanga (optional)	3 stalks scallions, cut into 1-inch pieces
	1 cup chopped fresh dill

In a mini chopper add lemongrass and chop 10 seconds. Add garlic, shallot and pepper. Chop another 10 seconds.

Heat a large pot with oil on high heat. Add lemongrass, garlic, onion, and pepper mixture, kalanga, and kaffir lime leaves. Stir constantly until light brown, 3 minutes. Add chicken and stir constantly 3 minutes. Add salt and fish sauce.

Stir constantly another 3 minutes, allowing the chicken to absorb the flavor. Add spinach and 2 cans of water (use the empty spinach can). Mix well and bring to a boil. Turn the heat to low, cover, and simmer 20 minutes. Stir occasionally.

Turn the heat to high and add scallions and dill. Mix well and transfer to a serving bowl.

Serve with rice, lettuce of any kind, cucumber, or Napa cabbage.

SERVES 4

Yellow Curry Chicken

GANG GALI

2 tablespoons olive oil	2 tablespoons fish sauce
1½ tablespoons yellow curry powder	1 tablespoon sugar (optional)
	1 can (13.5 ounces) coconut milk
1 pound boneless chicken breast, sliced in bite-size pieces	1½ cups cubed white potatoes
	1½ cups cubed sweet potatoes
1 teaspoon salt	

Heat a wok or large pot with oil on high heat. Add curry powder and mix well 3 seconds. Add chicken and stir constantly 30 seconds. Add salt, fish sauce and sugar. Stir constantly another 30 seconds, allowing the chicken to absorb the flavor.

Add coconut milk and stir well. Cover and bring to a boil. Add white and sweet potatoes and stir well. Cover and cook 8 minutes, stirring occasionally. Transfer to a serving bowl and serve with rice.

SERVES 2

Grilled or Roasted Chicken

PING GICE

¼ cup sliced lemongrass, cut across the grain	¼ cup sugar
1 head garlic	¼ cup soy sauce
1 teaspoon black pepper	1 (4-pound) chicken, whole or quartered
1 teaspoon salt	

In a blender, combine lemongrass, garlic, pepper, salt, sugar, and soy sauce. Blend 15 seconds. Place chicken in a large plastic bag and add blended mixture.

Let out the air and close the bag. Coat the chicken with the mixture. Refrigerate at least 2 hours or overnight.

Preheat the oven to 400 degrees and roast the whole chicken for 1½ to 2 hours. If quartered, grill 20 minutes on each side, or broil in the oven 30 minutes on each side.

Serve with rice, steamed vegetables, and tomato sauce.

SERVES 4

Grilled Pork

PING MOU

2 pounds boneless pork	2 tablespoons oyster sauce
2 tablespoons sugar	1 teaspoon ground white pepper
1 teaspoon salt	1 teaspoon garlic powder
2 tablespoons soy sauce	

Cut pork in strips ½ inch thick and 1 inch wide. Place in a large plastic bag.

Add sugar, salt, soy sauce, oyster sauce, pepper, and garlic powder. Let the air out and close the bag. Coat the pork with seasonings and refrigerate overnight.

The following day, grill the pork until light brown, 10 minutes on each side, or broil in the oven for 15 minutes each side.

Serve with sticky rice, tomato sauce, and steamed vegetables.

SERVES 2

Penn's Fried Meatballs

JEUNE LOUK SEEN

¼ cup sliced lemongrass, cut across the grain (optional)	1 tablespoon soy sauce (optional)
6 cloves garlic	1 tablespoon sugar (optional)
1 large onion, sliced	1 teaspoon ground black pepper
1 pound ground pork or turkey	2 stalks scallions, chopped
½ teaspoon salt	½ cup chopped cilantro
1 tablespoon fish sauce (optional)	3 cups vegetable oil

In a mini chopper add lemongrass and chop 10 seconds. Add garlic, and onion, and chop another 10 seconds. Transfer to a large mixing bowl and add pork, salt, fish sauce, soy sauce, sugar, pepper, scallions and cilantro. Mix well with your hands (use gloves if desired). Form 3 tablespoons into a ball and place on wax paper. Repeat until all the meat is used.

Heat a frying pan with oil on high heat. Drop in the meatballs, one at a time. Fry until golden brown, about 8 minutes each side. Place on paper towels to absorb the oil.

You can also brush with oil and broil in oven until golden brown, about 10 minutes each side.

Serve with rice, steamed vegetables, and tomato sauce or mashed eggplant.

SERVES 2

Orange Pork

YUM MOU

1 pound lean boneless pork	1 tablespoon fish sauce
1½ teaspoons salt	1 tablespoon lime juice
1 tablespoon soy sauce	1 teaspoon sugar (optional)
½ teaspoon ground white pepper	2 red chili peppers, chopped
1 tablespoon honey	(optional)
1 tablespoon fresh orange zest	1 orange, peeled and cubed
2 tablespoons freshly squeezed	1 stalk scallion, chopped
orange juice	½ cup chopped cilantro
¼ cup julienned fresh ginger	3 leaves romaine lettuce for garnish
1 small red onion, sliced	½ cup roasted cashew nuts

Cut pork in strip ½ inch thick and 1 inch wide. Place pork in a large plastic bag. Add ½ teaspoon salt, soy sauce, white pepper, honey, orange zest, and orange juice. Coat the pork with seasoning and refrigerate 2 hours.

Grill the pork until light brown, 10 minutes each side, or broil in the oven 15 minutes on each side. Let it cool 10 minutes.

Thinly sliced the pork and transfer to a large mixing bowl. Add ginger, onion, 1 teaspoon salt, fish sauce, lime juice, sugar, and hot peppers. Mix well with a spoon. Add orange, scallion, and cilantro and mix lightly.

Place romaine leaves on a serving plate with the stems touching each other in the center and ends pointing out. Transfer the mixture on the center of the plate and sprinkle with cashew nuts.

Serve at room temperature with rice.

SERVES 2

Pureed Turkey with Roasted Garlic

PONE GAI GUANG

This dish is very healthful and easy to make, and it tastes great.

1 head garlic	1 pound ground turkey
5 shallots or 1 medium onion, sliced	1 tablespoons salt
	2 stalks scallions, chopped
2 large hot peppers or 1 small bell pepper for a non-spicy dish	½ cup chopped cilantro

Preheat oven on broil. Place garlic, shallots and peppers on a tray. Broil 8 minutes on each side. Turn off the heat and let them sit inside the oven another 10 minutes.

In a medium pot, bring 1 cup water to a boil.

Form ground turkey into 4 balls. Drop in the boiling water and add salt.

Cover and cook 15 minutes. Keep warm and set aside.

In a food processor, add garlic, shallots and peppers. Chop 5 seconds. Add turkey and broth and chop 10 seconds. Add scallions and ⅔ of the cilantro and mix lightly.

Transfer to a serving bowl and sprinkle with the remaining cilantro for garnish.

Serve at room temperature with rice, fresh cucumber slices, or steamed vegetables.

SERVES 4

Roasted Duck

OPE PIT

This dish needs to marinate for two days, so plan ahead.

1 whole duck	3 tablespoons sugar
¼ cup soy sauce	1 teaspoon ground white pepper
10 star anise	1 teaspoon garlic powder
1 teaspoon salt	

To clean and bone the duck: Cut along the spine from neck to tail and slowly fillet the meat off the bone, leaving the skin on the breast and legs. Save the bones, neck, wings, liver and kidneys to make Rice in Duck Broth (page 72). If you don't want to make the Rice in Duck Broth, marinate the whole duck.

Mix the soy sauce, star anise, salt, sugar, pepper and garlic.

Place the cut up duck or the whole duck in a resealable plastic bag. Pour in the mixture, let out the air and close the bag. Coat the duck with mixture and refrigerate for 2 nights. Turn the bag over after one night to marinate the other side.

Preheat the oven to 375 degrees. Discard the star anise and excess marinade. Place the duck on a rack over a roasting pan. Add 4 cups water in the roasting pan to avoid burning the drippings. Roast for 1 hour if you like it medium-well or 2 hours if you like it crispy.

SERVES 2 TO 4

Steamed Chicken

MOKE GICE

¼ cup rice
¼ cup sliced lemongrass, cut
    across the grain
6 cloves garlic
3 shallots, sliced
1 large hot pepper, sliced or ¼ bell
    pepper for a non-spicy dish
1 pound boneless chicken breast,
    cut in bite-size pieces

½ teaspoon salt
2 tablespoons fish sauce (optional)
1 large egg
3 kaffir limes leaves, minced
    (optional)
2 stalks scallions, chopped

Soak the rice in warm water for 30 minutes.

In a blender, add rice, lemongrass, and ½ cup water. Blend 10 seconds. Add garlic, shallots and pepper. Blend another 10 seconds. Transfer to a large mixing bowl. Add chicken, salt, fish sauce, egg, kaffir lime leaves and scallions. Mix well with a spoon.

Transfer to a round or square baking pan, and cover tightly with foil. Steam on high heat for 45 minutes or bake in 375 degrees oven for 1 hour.

Serve with rice and steamed vegetables.

SERVES 2

Steamed Ground Turkey with Kaffir Lime Leaves

MOKE GICE GUANG

¼ cup rice	1 pound ground turkey
¼ cup sliced lemongrass, cut across the grain	2 large eggs
6 cloves garlic	½ teaspoon salt
4 shallots or 1 small onion, sliced	2 stalks scallions, chopped
1 can (2 ounces) anchovies	4 kaffir lime leaves, minced (optional)
1 large hot pepper, sliced or ¼ bell pepper for a non-spicy dish	

Soak the rice in warm water for 30 minutes

In a blender, add rice, lemongrass, and ½ cup water. Blend 10 seconds. Add garlic, shallots, anchovies, and hot pepper. Blend another 10 seconds. Transfer to a large mixing bowl. Add turkey, eggs, salt, scallions and kaffir lime leaves. Mix well with spoon.

Transfer to a round or square baking pan. Cover tightly with aluminum foil and steam on high heat for 45 minutes or bake in 375 degrees oven for 1 hour.

Cut in 4 pieces and serve with rice and steamed vegetables.

SERVES 4

Steamed Ground Turkey with Cellophane Noodles

NUNGE GICE GUANG

1 package (1.7 ounces) cellophane noodles	1 teaspoon ground black pepper
6 cloves garlic	½ teaspoon salt
3 shallots or 1 small onion, sliced	2 tablespoons fish sauce
1 pound ground turkey	2 stalks scallions, chopped
2 large eggs	

Soak cellophane noodles in warm water 10 minutes and cut in 3-inch pieces.

In a blender combine garlic, shallot and ¼ cup water, chop 10 seconds. Transfer to a large mixing bowl. Add turkey, eggs, pepper, noodles, salt, fish sauce, and scallions. Mix well with a spoon.

Transfer to a round or square baking pan. Cover tightly with aluminum foil and steam on high heat for 45 minutes or bake in 375 degrees oven for 1 hour.

Cut in 4 pieces and serve with rice and steamed vegetables.

SERVES 4

Steamed Stuffed Cornish Hen

NUNGE GICE NOY

2 tablespoons soy sauce	½ cup sliced fresh button
½ teaspoon ground black pepper	mushrooms
2 whole Cornish hens	½ teaspoon salt
	½ teaspoon ground black pepper
STUFFING:	2 tablespoons soy sauce
1 package (1.7 ounces) cellophane	1 stalk scallion, chopped
noodles	½ cup chopped cilantro
¼ cup sliced dried wood ear	¼ cup chopped roasted peanuts
mushrooms (optional)	
½ cup sliced fresh shiitake	
mushrooms	

Rub soy sauce and black pepper on the hens and set aside.

FOR THE STUFFING: Soak cellophane noodles in warm water 10 minutes. Drain well and cut in 3-inch pieces. Soak wood ear mushrooms in hot water 30 minutes and drain well.

In a large mixing bowl, combine noodles, wood ear, shiitake and button mushrooms, salt, pepper, soy sauce, scallions, cilantro, and peanuts. Mix well and stuff the mixture inside the hens. Leave the hens in the bowl, cover with plastic wrap, and refrigerate overnight.

Transfer the hens to a baking pan and cover tightly with foil. Steam on high heat for 1½ hours or bake in 375 degrees oven for 2 hours.

Serve with rice and Ginger Sauce (page 58).

SERVES 4

Stuffed Cabbage

MOKE GALUM

¼ cup rice	½ tablespoon salt
¼ cup sliced lemongrass (optional), cut across the grain	2 tablespoons fish sauce (optional)
6 cloves garlic	2 stalks scallions, chopped
3 shallots or 1 small onion, sliced	½ cup chopped fresh dill
1 large hot pepper, sliced or ¼ bell pepper for a non-spicy dish	1 medium green cabbage
1 pound ground pork, beef, or turkey	

Soak rice in warm water for 30 minutes.

In a blender, add rice, lemongrass, and ¼ cup water. Blend 10 seconds. Add garlic, shallots, and pepper. Blend another 10 seconds. Transfer to a large mixing bowl. Add pork, salt, fish sauce, scallions and dill. Mix well with both hands and set aside.

Fill a large pot ⅔ full with water and bring to a boil. Drop in the whole cabbage head for a minute to soften the leaves. Take the cabbage out, cut the stem, and peel one or two leaves off. Repeat the whole process 2 more times to get 6 leaves. Quarter the remaining cabbage and set aside.

Lay a cabbage leaf on a plate and spoon ⅙ of the mixture on the center. Fold left and right sides toward the middle and fold in both ends. Place the stuffed cabbages with seam down on a baking dish. Cover tightly with aluminum foil. Steam for 45 minutes on high heat. Add the remaining cabbage on the side of the pan and steam another 15 minutes or roast in a 375-degree oven for 1 hour.

Transfer to a serving plate and garnish with sprigs of dill. Serve hot with rice and steamed vegetables.

SERVES 4

Stuffed Pepper

MOKE MOCK PIT

¼ cup rice	1 pound ground pork, beef, or
6 large bell peppers	turkey
¼ cup sliced lemongrass	½ tablespoon salt
6 cloves garlic	2 tablespoons fish sauce (optional)
3 shallots or 1 small onion, sliced	2 stalks scallions, chopped
1 large hot pepper, sliced or ¼ bell	½ cup chopped fresh dill
pepper for a non-spicy dish	

Soak the rice in warm water for 30 minutes

Cut off the top of the bell peppers, scrape out the seeds, and set aside.

In a blender, add rice, lemongrass, and ¼ cup water. Blend 10 seconds. Add garlic, shallots, and pepper. Blend another 10 seconds. Transfer to a large mixing bowl. Add pork, salt, fish sauce, scallions and dill. Mix well with a spoon.

Spoon ⅙ of the mixture in each pepper and spread it evenly. Place the peppers in a baking dish and cover tightly with aluminum foil. Steam 1 hour on high heat or roast in a 375-degree oven for 1 hour. Serve with rice and steamed vegetables.

SERVES 4

Steak

You can choose any kind of meat your desire. You can marinate it in strips or whole.

1 pound London broil	½ teaspoon salt
2 tablespoons sliced lemongrass, cut across the grain	½ tablespoon sugar (optional)
	1 tablespoon fish sauce
6 cloves garlic	1 tablespoon soy sauce
1 teaspoon ground black pepper	

Cut the meat into 1-inch thick strips, place in a resealable plastic bag, and set aside.

In a blender, add lemongrass and ¼ cup water. Blend 10 seconds. Add garlic, pepper, salt, sugar, fish sauce, and soy sauce. Blend another 10 seconds. Pour on the meat, let out the air out and close the bag. Coat the meat with the mixture. Refrigerate 2 hours or overnight. Turn the bag over to marinate the other side halfway through the process.

Grill on high heat for 5 minutes each side or longer if you desire, or broil in the oven for 10 minutes each side.

Serve hot with rice, steamed vegetables, and Tomato Sauce (page 65) or Sweet and Sour Sauce (page 64).

SERVES 2

Lob

Lob is a traditional Laotian dish. We serve lob on holidays and special occasions. It is one of the few dishes that are served with wine. Lob can be made with chicken, fish, duck, and wild game. The most common lob is beef. It is always served with sticky rice and accompanied with fresh and bitter vegetables such as lettuce of any kind, green cabbage, Chinese cabbage, bok choy, cucumber, cauliflower, radish, long green beans, watercress, mustard greens, broccoli rape, escarole, and grilled bitter melon.

THE PREPARATION VARIES DEPENDING ON THE MEAT USED:
- fish lob is made raw.
- beef lob is made raw to medium-well.
- wild game lob is cooked medium-well.
- chicken lob is cooked just about well done, but not too well done.

Whatever kind of meat you decide to use must be fresh and very lean. Mincing it yourself is recommended, but if you must, use extra-lean ground beef, chicken, or turkey. Before you start, make sure you have rice powder.

Rice Powder

KOA KORE

Rice powder is so easy to make that even a beginner can look like a pro.

Put ½ cup plain uncooked rice in an old unwanted pan. Place on top of the stove on high heat. Stir and shake the pan occasionally until the rice is dark brown, 8 minutes. I recommend doing this outside on a grill in the summer because it creates a lot of smoke. Let cool 10 minutes. Transfer to a coffee grinder and grind until it turns to powder, 15 seconds. Store in an airtight container for a few months or refrigerate up to a year.

MAKES ⅓ CUP

Beef Lob

LOB SEEN

1 pound extra-lean ground beef	1 teaspoon kalanga powder
2 tablespoons lime or lemon juice	2 kaffir lime leaves, minced
½ teaspoon salt	1 tablespoon rice powder (page 113)
1½ tablespoons fish sauce	1 stalk scallion, chopped
½ teaspoon crushed hot pepper	½ cup chopped cilantro
(optional)	½ cup chopped mint

Cook ground beef in a nonstick pan (do not use oil) on medium heat. Stir constantly and cook to your desire, rare to medium well. Let cool 10 minutes.

Transfer to a large mixing bowl, add lime juice, salt, fish sauce, pepper, kalanga powder, kaffir lime leaves, and rice powder. Crumble the meat with both hands (use gloves if desired) and mix well. Add scallion, cilantro, and mint and mix lightly so as not to bruise the herbs.

Accompany with fresh vegetables and serve with sticky rice.

SERVES 2

Chicken Lob

LOB GICE

1 pound extra-lean ground chicken or turkey	1 teaspoon kalanga powder
2 tablespoons lime or lemon juice	2 kaffir lime leaves, minced
½ teaspoon salt	1 tablespoon rice powder (page 113)
1½ tablespoons fish sauce	1 stalk scallion, chopped
½ teaspoon crushed hot pepper (optional)	½ cup chopped cilantro
	½ cup chopped mint

Cook the chicken in nonstick wok (do not use oil) on medium heat. Stir constantly until the chicken is just about cooked, 10 minutes (do not brown or overcook).

Transfer to a large mixing bowl and let cool 10 minutes. Add lime juice, salt, fish sauce, pepper, kalanga powder, kaffir lime leaves, and rice powder. Crumble the meat with both hands (use gloves if desired) and mix well. Add scallion, cilantro, and mint. Mix lightly so as not to bruise the herbs.

Accompany with fresh vegetables and serve with sticky rice.

SERVES 2

Duck Lob

LOB PIT

1 whole duck	4 kaffir lime leaves, minced
½ teaspoon salt	2 tablespoons rice powder (page
1 tablespoon lime or lemon juice	113)
1 teaspoon salt	2 stalks scallions, chopped
3 tablespoons fish sauce	¾ cup chopped cilantro
1 teaspoon crushed hot pepper	¾ cup chopped mint
2 teaspoons kalanga powder	

To clean and bone the duck: Cut along the spine from neck to tail and slowly skin the duck. Fillet the meat off the bone and trim the fat. Save the bones, neck, wings, liver and kidney to make Duck Soup (page 33).

Preheat oven to broil. Sprinkle salt on the duck meat and place on a baking pan. Broil on medium well, 6 minutes each side, or grill on medium heat 5 minutes each side. Let cool 10 minutes.

Cut the meat in strips ¼ inch wide and ½ inch thick and mince into very small pieces. Transfer to a large mixing bowl. Add lime juice, salt, fish sauce, pepper, kalanga powder, kaffir lime leaves, and rice powder. Mix well with both hands (use gloves if desired). Add scallions, cilantro, and mint. Mix lightly so as not to bruise the herbs.

Accompany with fresh vegetables and serve at room temperature with sticky rice.

SERVES 4

Pork Lob

LOB MOU

1 pound extra-lean ground pork	2 kaffir lime leaves, minced
2 tablespoons lime or lemon juice	1 tablespoon rice powder (page 113)
½ teaspoon salt	1 tablespoon thinly sliced
1½ tablespoons fish sauce	lemongrass, cut across the grain
½ teaspoon crushed hot pepper	2 stalk scallion, chopped
(optional)	½ cup chopped cilantro
1 teaspoon kalanga powder	½ cup chopped mint

Cook the pork in a nonstick wok (do not use oil) on medium heat. Stir constantly until the pork is just about cooked, 10 minutes. Do not overcook.

Transfer to a large mixing bowl and let cool 10 minutes. Add lime juice, salt, fish sauce, pepper, kalanga powder, kaffir lime leaves, rice powder, and lemongrass. Crumble the meat with both hands (use gloves if desired) and mix well. Add scallions, cilantro, and mint. Mix lightly so as not to bruise the herbs.

Accompany with fresh vegetables and serve with sticky rice.

SERVES 2

Raw Fish Lob

LOB PA

1 pound lean fresh fish fillet (preferably striped bass)	1½ teaspoons kalanga powder
4 tablespoons lime or lemon juice	3 kaffir lime leaves, minced
¼ cup thinly sliced fresh lemon-grass, cut across the grain	1 tablespoon rice powder (page 113)
	2 shallots, thinly sliced
½ teaspoon salt	3 cloves garlic, sliced
1½ tablespoons fish sauce	2 stalks scallions, chopped
½ teaspoon crushed hot pepper (optional)	½ cup chopped cilantro
	½ cup chopped mint

Cut the fish in ½-inch strips and slice very thin. Transfer to a large mixing bowl and add lime juice. Mix well and let it set 3 minutes. Strain and squeeze out the juice from the fish in a small pan and place the fish in a clean bowl.

OPTIONAL: Cook the fish juice on medium heat until it reduces to ¼ cup, about 8 minutes. Let cool 5 minutes and add it to the fish for extra flavor.

In the bowl containing the fish, add lemongrass, salt, fish sauce, pepper, kalanga powder, kaffir lime leaves, rice powder, shallots, and garlic. Mix well with both hands (use gloves if desired). Add scallions, cilantro, and mint. Mix lightly so as not to bruise the herbs.

Serve with fresh vegetables, sticky rice, and Fish Soup (page 35).

SERVES 2

Sautés

When sautéing, you want to get intense flavors (the flavor should stay on the meat and vegetables). The heat must be extremely high to sear the meat, fish, or poultry. If the heat is not hot enough, the juices will seep out and create too much water, which will result in the dish losing its flavor.

There are three ways to retain the intense flavor when your stove cannot create enough heat:

- Cook your meat, fish, or poultry until almost done (at 90 percent of desired doneness) and take it out, leaving the juices to cook until they evaporate. Add the meat, fish, or poultry back in and then add flavors such as salt, fish, sauce, soy sauce, or oyster sauce. This way your meat, fish, or poultry is still moist (not overcooked).

- After adding meat, fish, or poultry, cook until the juices evaporate and then add flavors such as salt, fish sauce, soy sauce, or oyster sauce.

- Cook for only 2 to 4 people a time.

Hot Pepper Beef

KORE MOCK PIT

This dish is great for people who like spicy food. For people who do not, substitute hot peppers with bell peppers.

2 tablespoons olive oil	½ teaspoon salt
1 head garlic, chopped	1½ tablespoons fish sauce
1 pound lean beef, thinly sliced in bite-size pieces	6 jalapeno peppers or large hot peppers, sliced

Heat a wok with oil on high heat. Add garlic and stir constantly until light brown, 3 minutes. Add beef and peppers. Stir constantly to cook the beef to medium doneness, 3 minutes. Add salt and fish sauce. Stir well 2 minutes and turn off the heat.

Transfer to a serving plate and serve with rice.

SERVES 2

Beef with Mushroom and Asparagus

KORE HIT ASPARAGUS

There are no asparagus in Laos. We call it American bamboo shoot.

2 tablespoons oil	1 tablespoon soy sauce
6 cloves garlic, chopped	2 tablespoons oyster sauce
1 pound beef, thinly sliced in	1 tablespoon sugar (optional)
bite-size pieces	1 pound asparagus, trimmed
½ teaspoon salt	½ pound mushrooms, quartered

Heat a wok with oil on high heat. Add garlic and stir constantly until light brown, 3 minutes. Add beef and stir constantly 30 seconds. Add salt, soy sauce, oyster sauce, and sugar. Stir constantly another 30 seconds, allowing the beef to absorb the flavor. Take the beef out while it is still medium done.

Cook the juice until thickened. Add asparagus and mushrooms. Stir well and cook 3 minutes. Add the beef back in, and stir well 1 minute.

Transfer to a serving plate and serve with rice and hot sauce.

SERVES 2

Beef with Zucchini

KORE MOCK UR YAO

There were no zucchini in Laos, so young butternut squash were used for this dish. They taste almost the same. When I first came to the United States, I thought that zucchini was such a cute vegetable; I called it "long young squash."

1 pound zucchini	1 tablespoon soy sauce
2 tablespoons olive oil	1 tablespoon oyster sauce
1 head garlic, chopped	½ tablespoon sugar (optional)
½ pound lean beef, thinly sliced in bite-size pieces	2 stalks scallions, chopped
	1 cup chopped cilantro
½ teaspoon salt	

Slice zucchini in 4 pieces lengthwise. Lay 2 slices on top of each other and cut on angle ¼ inch thick.

Heat a wok with oil on high heat. Add garlic and stir constantly until light brown, 2 minutes. Add beef and stir constantly 2 minutes. Add salt, soy sauce, oyster sauce, and sugar. Stir another minute, until the beef reaches medium doneness. Add zucchini and stir constantly 2 minutes. Add scallions, stir well, and turn off the heat. Add cilantro, stir well, transfer to a serving plate, and serve with rice.

SERVES 2

Ground Turkey with Eggplant

KORE MOCK KURE

My sister Lika came to the United States eight months before me. When she first introduced me to eggplant, I was impressed with its size but was sure it was inedible. I was wrong; it is quite good made this way.

2 tablespoons olive oil	1 medium eggplant, peeled and
6 cloves garlic, chopped	sliced in bite-size pieces
1 small onion, chopped	1 large hot pepper, sliced (optional)
½ pound ground turkey	2 stalks scallions, chopped
½ teaspoon salt	1 cup chopped cilantro or basil
2 tablespoons fish sauce	leaves

Heat a wok with oil on high heat. Add garlic and onion. Stir constantly until light brown, 3 minutes. Add ground turkey and stir constantly until all juices evaporate, 5 minutes. Add salt and fish sauce. Stir another minute, allowing the turkey to absorb the flavor. Add eggplant and pepper. Cook 5 minutes, stirring occasionally. Add scallions, stir well, and turn off the heat. Add cilantro or basil and stir well.

Transfer to a serving plate and serve with rice.

SERVES 2

Pork with Bean Sprouts

KORE TORE GALK

When I was a child, I couldn't eat bean sprouts. I felt sick even if I just had a tiny piece in my food. Now I love them; they are so refreshing.

2 tablespoons olive oil	1 tablespoon oyster sauce
6 cloves garlic, chopped	1 tablespoon sugar (optional)
1 pound boneless pork, thinly	1 pound bean sprouts
sliced in bite-size pieces	1 medium ripe tomato, sliced
½ teaspoon salt	2 stalks scallions, chopped
1 tablespoon soy sauce	1 cup chopped cilantro

Heat a wok with oil on high heat. Add garlic and stir constantly until light brown, 3 minutes. Add pork and stir constantly for 5 minutes. Add salt, soy sauce, oyster sauce, and sugar. Stir constantly 2 minutes, allowing the pork to absorb the flavor. Add bean sprouts and stir well. Add tomato and scallion. Stir well and turn off the heat. Add cilantro and stir well.

Transfer to a serving plate and serve with rice.

SERVES 2

Pork with Bok Choy

KORE PUCK GOT KAO

Bok choy in Laos was less than half the size it is here in the United States, and did not form a very tight head.

Bok choy contains a lot of water. Make sure that your pan is extremely hot and prepare only 2 servings at a time at the most. Preparing one serving at a time would be best.

2 tablespoons olive oil	2 tablespoons oyster sauce
6 cloves garlic, chopped	1 tablespoon sugar (optional)
1 pound boneless pork, thinly	4 cups sliced bok choy
sliced in bite-size pieces	2 stalks scallions, chopped
1 tablespoon soy sauce	1 cup chopped cilantro

Heat a wok with oil on high heat. Add garlic and stir constantly until light brown, 2 minutes. Add pork and stir constantly for 5 minutes. Add soy sauce, oyster sauce, and sugar. Stir constantly 2 minutes, allowing the pork to absorb the flavor. Add bok choy and stir well 2 minutes. Add scallions, stir well, and turn off the heat. Add cilantro and stir well.

Transfer to a serving plate and serve with rice and hot sauce.

SERVES 2

Pork with Cabbage

KORE GALUM

Cabbage is a vegetable I couldn't eat when I was a child. I wanted to learn to eat it because it was not cheap. It was a seasonal vegetable that did not grow well in certain areas, especially my town. When the season came, everybody ate cabbage with papaya salad, but I could not bring it near my nose. I guess the smell of vegetables disappears when you grow older. I love it now.

Cabbage is great for sautéing because it does not contain a lot of water. It remains crispy and intensely flavorful after cooking. Leave out the pork or substitute with tofu if you are a vegetarian.

2 tablespoons olive oil	2 tablespoons oyster sauce
6 cloves garlic, chopped	1 tablespoon sugar (optional)
1 pound pork, thinly sliced in bite-size pieces	4 cups sliced green cabbage
1 tablespoon soy sauce	

Heat a wok with oil on high heat. Add garlic and stir constantly until light brown, 2 minutes. Add pork, stir and cook for 5 minutes. Add soy sauce, oyster sauce, and sugar. Stir 2 minutes, allowing the pork to absorb the flavor. Add cabbage and stir well 3 minutes.

Transfer to serving plate and serve with rice and hot sauce.

SERVES 2

Pork with Cauliflower

KORE DALK GALUM

Cauliflower was expensive in Laos because it did not grow well there. It was one fourth of the size it is in the United States and had a stronger flavor. The taste was a little too strong for me, but it was manageable because we rarely ate it. When I first saw cauliflower in the United States, I was very impressed with its size and the quantity available, and now I can eat it raw.

2 tablespoons olive oil	2 tablespoons oyster sauce
1 head garlic, chopped	1 tablespoon sugar (optional)
1 pound boneless pork, thinly sliced in bite-size pieces	3 cups sliced cauliflower
	2 stalks scallions, chopped
1 tablespoon soy sauce	1 cup chopped cilantro

Heat a wok with oil on high heat. Add garlic and stir constantly until light brown, 2 minutes. Add pork, and stir, and cook for 2 minutes. Add soy sauce, oyster sauce, and sugar. Stir another minute, allowing the pork to absorb the flavor.

Add cauliflower and stir to cook 4 minutes. Add scallions, stir well, and turn off the heat. Add cilantro and stir well.

Transfer to a serving plate and serve with rice and hot sauce.

SERVES 2

Pork with Cucumber

KORE MOCK TANG

I love the Kirby cucumbers that are so abundant in Laos. When my sister Lika showed me my first American cucumber, I was impressed with its appearance. I had problems with the taste at first: It didn't taste quite as good as the ones in Laos, probably because it had been refrigerated.

2 pounds Kirby cucumbers	2 tablespoons oyster sauce
2 tablespoons olive oil	1 tablespoon sugar (optional)
1 head garlic, chopped	1 medium tomato, sliced
1 pound ground pork	2 stalks scallions, chopped
1 tablespoon soy sauce	1 cup chopped cilantro

Peel and halve the cucumbers lengthwise (remove the seeds if they are old). Slice ¼ inch thick and set aside.

Heat a wok with oil on high heat. Add garlic and stir until light brown, 2 minutes. Add pork, stir, and cook for 5 minutes. Add soy sauce, oyster sauce, and sugar. Stir another minute, allowing the pork to absorb the flavor. Add cucumber and stir constantly 2 minutes. Add tomato and scallions. Stir well and turn off the heat. Add cilantro and stir lightly.

Transfer to a serving plate and serve with rice and hot sauce.

SERVES 2

Pork with Green Beans

KORE MOCK TORE KACK

Green beans are abundant in Laos. We eat them sautéed, boiled, or steamed.

2 tablespoons olive oil	2 tablespoons oyster sauce
6 cloves garlic, chopped	1 tablespoon sugar (optional)
1 pound pork, thinly sliced in bite-size pieces	1 pound green beans, cut 1 inch long or French cut
1 tablespoon soy sauce	

Heat a wok with oil on high heat. Add garlic and stir constantly until light brown, 2 minutes. Add pork, stir, and cook for 3 minutes. Add soy sauce, oyster sauce, and sugar. Stir another minute, allowing the pork to absorb the flavor. Add beans and stir well. Cover and cook 3 minutes.

Take the cover off to avoid too much water. Continue stirring and cook another 3 minutes, until the beans are cooked but still crispy.

Transfer to a serving plate and serve with rice and hot sauce.

SERVES 2

Red Curry with Green Beans

KORE MOCK TORE KUANG GANG PIT

2 tablespoons olive oil	1 tablespoon fish sauce
1 tablespoon red curry paste	1 tablespoon sugar (optional)
1 pound boneless pork, thinly sliced in bite-size pieces	2 kaffir lime leaves, minced (optional)
1 teaspoon salt	1 pound green beans, cut 1 inch long

Heat a wok with oil on high heat. Add curry paste and stir well for a minute. Add pork, stir, and cook for 3 minutes. Add salt, fish sauce, sugar, and kaffir lime leaves. Stir another minute, allowing the pork to absorb the flavor. Add beans and stir well. Cover and cook 3 minutes.

Take the cover off to avoid too much water. Continue stirring and cook another 3 minutes, until the beans are cooked but still crispy.

Transfer to a serving plate and serve with rice.

SERVES 2

Pork with Mushrooms and Green Beans

KORE HIT MOCK TORE KACK

There were no button mushrooms in Laos, only straw and wild mushrooms. They were expensive and had to be cooked before eating. I was thrilled when my sister Lika told me that button mushrooms are available year-round in the United States and can be eaten raw. I love all kinds of mushrooms. This Laotian recipe works well with button mushrooms.

2 tablespoons olive oil	½ pound green beans, cut 1 inch long
6 cloves garlic, chopped	
1 pound pork, thinly sliced in bite-size pieces	½ pound button mushrooms, sliced or quartered
1 tablespoon soy sauce	1 medium tomato, sliced
2 tablespoons oyster sauce	2 stalks scallions, chopped
1 tablespoon sugar (optional)	½ cup chopped cilantro

Heat a wok with oil on high heat. Add garlic and stir constantly until light brown, 2 minutes. Add pork, stir, and cook for 3 minutes. Add soy sauce, oyster sauce, and sugar. Stir another minute, allowing the pork to absorb the flavor. Add beans and stir well. Cover and cook 3 minutes. Add mushrooms and stir well for 3 minutes. Add the tomato and scallions. Stir well and turn off the heat. Add cilantro and stir lightly.

Transfer to a serving plate and serve with rice and hot sauce.

SERVES 2

Pork with Mushrooms and Snow Peas

KORE HIT MOCK TORE YUD

There were not many snow peas in Laos and they were expensive. I love snow peas in a soup or a sauté.

2 tablespoons olive oil	2 tablespoons oyster sauce
6 cloves garlic, chopped	1 tablespoon sugar (optional)
1 pound pork, thinly sliced in bite-size pieces	½ pound snow peas, stemmed
1 tablespoon soy sauce	½ pound fresh button mushrooms, sliced or quartered

Heat a wok with oil on high heat. Add garlic and stir constantly until light brown, 2 minutes. Add pork, stir, and cook for 5 minutes. Add soy sauce, oyster sauce, and sugar. Stir another minute, allowing the pork to absorb the flavor. Add snow peas and mushrooms. Stir constantly 3 minutes.

Transfer to a serving plate and serve with rice and hot sauce.

SERVES 2

Portabella Pork

KORE HIT YICE

There were no portabella mushrooms in Laos but there were straw mushrooms, which I used for this dish.

2 tablespoons olive oil	1 tablespoon sugar (optional)
6 cloves garlic, chopped	6 ounces portabella, sliced in
1 pound pork, sliced in bite-size	bite-size pieces
pieces	1 sweet onion, sliced
1 tablespoons soy sauce	½ cup chopped cilantro
2 tablespoons oyster sauce	

Heat a wok with oil on high heat. Add garlic and stir constantly until light brown, 2 minutes. Add pork, stir, and cook for 5 minutes. Add soy sauce, oyster sauce, and sugar. Stir another minute, allowing the pork to absorb the flavor. Add portabella and stir well 3 minutes. Add onion, stir well another minute, and turn off the heat. Add cilantro and stir lightly.

Transfer to a serving plate and serve with rice and hot sauce.

SERVES 2

Eggs

Eggs with Bean Sprouts

KORE KICE TORE GALK

I love bean sprouts and put them in every dish that I can!

1 cup bean sprouts	1 teaspoon salt
3 large eggs	1 tablespoon soy sauce
1 stalk scallion, chopped	2 tablespoons olive oil
¼ cup chopped cilantro	4 cloves garlic, chopped

Heat a large frying pan on high heat. Add bean sprouts and stir constantly for a minute. Let cool 5 minutes.

Beat eggs in a mixing bowl. Add bean sprouts, scallion, cilantro, salt, and soy sauce and mix well.

Heat the same pan with oil on high heat. Add garlic and stir constantly until light brown, 2 minutes. Add egg mixture, pick up the pan and swirl it around to coat the pan evenly. Cook until light brown, 2 minutes. Turn over to cook the other side, 2 minutes.

Serve with rice and Sweet and Sour Sauce (page 64) for a quick meal.

SERVES 2

Eggs with Fresh Dill

KORE KICE PUCK SEE

Dill is always used fresh and is not expensive. It has a very strong flavor and does not go with many foods, so be careful when using it. A tiny bit of dill will change the flavor of a dish.

3 large eggs	1 tablespoon fish sauce
1 cup chopped fresh dill	2 tablespoons oil
1 stalk scallion, chopped	4 cloves garlic, chopped
½ teaspoon salt	

Beat eggs in a mixing bowl. Add dill, scallion, salt, and fish sauce. Mix well and set aside.

Heat a large frying pan with oil on high heat. Add garlic and stir constantly until light brown, 2 minutes. Add egg mixture, pick up the pan and swirl it around to coat the pan evenly. Cook until light brown, 2 minutes. Turn over to cook the other side, 2 minutes.

Serve with rice and hot sauce for a quick meal.

SERVES 2

Eggs with Mushroom

KORE KICE HIT

I love this dish with rice and Dried Pepper and Fish Sauce (page 56). I eat this a lot when I am by myself.

3 tablespoons olive oil	¼ cup chopped cilantro
1 cup sliced fresh button	½ teaspoon salt
mushrooms	1 tablespoon soy sauce
3 large eggs	2 tablespoons olive oil
1 stalk scallion, chopped	4 cloves garlic, chopped

Heat a large frying pan with 1 tablespoon oil on high heat. Add mushrooms and stir constantly 3 minutes. Let cool 5 minutes.

Beat the eggs in a medium mixing bowl. Add mushrooms, scallion, cilantro, salt, and soy sauce. Mix well and set aside.

Heat a large frying pan with 2 tablespoons oil on high heat. Add garlic and stir constantly until light brown, 2 minutes. Add egg mixture, pick up the pan and swirl it around to coat the pan evenly. Cook until light brown, 2 minutes. Turn over to cook the other side, 2 minutes.

Serve with rice and hot sauce for a quick meal.

SERVES 2

Eggs with Shrimp

KORE KICE GOUNG

Laos is a landlocked country. There were only freshwater shrimp, which were very small. We ate them with their shells on.

3 large eggs	1 teaspoon salt
½ cup shrimp, cooked and peeled	1 tablespoon soy sauce
1 stalk scallion, chopped	2 tablespoons olive oil
¼ cup chopped cilantro	4 cloves garlic, chopped

Beat eggs in a large mixing bowl. Add shrimp, scallion, cilantro, salt, and soy sauce. Mix well and set aside.

Heat a large frying pan with oil on high heat. Add garlic and stir constantly until light brown, 2 minutes. Add egg mixture, pick up the pan and swirl it around to coat the pan evenly. Cook until light brown, 2 minutes. Turn over to cook the other side, 2 minutes.

Serve with rice and hot sauce for a quick meal.

SERVES 2

Eggs with Tomato

TORE KICE MOCK LENT

I was amazed that so many American varieties of tomatoes are similar to the ones sold in Laos. It is wonderful that they are in markets all the time here.

3 large eggs	½ teaspoon salt
¼ cup chopped tomato	1 tablespoon soy sauce
1 stalk scallion, chopped	2 tablespoons olive oil
¼ cup chopped cilantro	4 cloves garlic, chopped

Beat the eggs in a large mixing bowl. Add the tomato, scallion, cilantro, salt, and soy sauce. Mix well and set aside.

Heat a large frying pan with oil on high heat. Add garlic, stir constantly until light brown, 2 minutes. Add egg mixture, pick up the pan and swirl it around to coat the pan evenly. Cook until light brown 2 minutes. Turn over to cook the other side, 2 minutes.

Serve with rice and hot sauce for a quick meal.

SERVES 2

Vegetarian
or Side Dishes

Bamboo with Fresh Herbs

YUM NALL MIKE

There were many varieties of bamboo in Laos and they grew wild. When in season, bamboo shoots were very cheap. Laotians eat a lot of bamboo shoots.

1 jar (24 ounces) julienned bamboo shoots in yanang extract	¼ cup julienned red bell pepper
½ teaspoon salt	¼ cup julienned red onion
1 tablespoon fish sauce (optional)	2 tablespoons lime juice
½ teaspoon crushed hot pepper (optional)	1 stalk scallion, chopped
	½ cup chopped cilantro

Open the bamboo jar and carefully pour out the water, saving only the thick green juice at the bottom, about ¼ cup. Shake well and transfer to a saucepan. Heat on medium heat 5 minutes.

Let cool 5 minutes and cut in 2-inch pieces. Transfer to a large mixing bowl. Add salt, fish sauce, hot pepper, red pepper, red onion, and lime juice. Mix well with a spoon. Add scallion and ¾ of the cilantro. Mix lightly and transfer to a serving plate.

Sprinkle with the remaining cilantro and serve with sticky rice or as a side dish with grilled chicken.

SERVES 2

Bamboo with Sesame Seeds

SUPE NALL MIKE

Bamboo shoots are mostly imported from Thailand, which is why they cost a little more here than they do in Laos. When I went back to Laos in 1994, I couldn't believe how wonderful the aroma of fresh bamboo shoots was, after being I had been deprived of it for 14 years. There is not much of aroma or taste left in canned bamboo.

¼ cup rice	½ teaspoon salt
1 jar (12 ounces) bamboo in yanang extract	1 tablespoon fish sauce (optional)
1 large hot pepper or ¼ bell pepper for a non-spicy dish	1 stalk scallion, chopped
	½ cup chopped cilantro

Soak the rice in warm water for 30 minutes. Open the bamboo jar carefully and drain, reserving only ½ cup of the thick green juice at the bottom. Cut the bamboo in 3-inch-long pieces.

Put sesame seeds in a frying pan and place on high heat. Shake and stir the seeds with a wooden spoon until light brown, 5 minutes. Let cool 5 minutes.

Grind in coffee grinder or blender 5 seconds and set aside.

In a blender, add rice, hot pepper, and ½ cup water. Blend 15 seconds and set aside.

Stir the reserved green juice well and transfer to a saucepan. Add the bamboo to the pan. Bring to a boil and add the rice mixture, salt, and fish sauce. Stir constantly 3 minutes. Let cool 10 minutes. Add scallion, cilantro, and ¾ of the sesame seeds. Mix lightly and transfer to a serving plate.

Sprinkle with the remaining sesame seeds and serve with sticky rice or as a side dish with grilled fish.

SERVES 2

Mashed Fried Eggplant

JAIL JEUNE MOCK KURE

My paternal grandmother grew many varieties of eggplants. I loved riding my bicycle to her farm to pick anything I wanted. All the vegetables she grew were for us, and there were a lot. After we had enough, she sold them for a little money. I miss one kind of eggplant that she grew. It was so crispy and sweet that you could eat it raw. She passed away a few months after I last visited her. She was the dearest person in my life.

Make sure to poke the whole peppers before frying, otherwise they will explode.

2 medium eggplants	1 teaspoon salt
3 cups vegetable oil	2 tablespoons fish sauce (optional)
1 medium onion, sliced	1 stalk scallion, chopped
1 head garlic, peeled	½ cup chopped cilantro
2 large hot peppers, or	
1 bell pepper, quartered,	
for a non-spicy dish	

Peel and slice the eggplants in wedges ¼ inch thick.

Heat oil in a frying pan or a wok on high heat. When the oil gets very hot, add garlic and onion. Fry until golden brown, 2 minutes each side. Place on paper towels to absorb the oil. Poke the hot pepper twice and fry until golden brown, 2 minutes on each side. Place on paper towels to absorb oil. Add 4 slices of eggplant at a time. Fry until golden brown, 3 minutes on each side. Lay each slice on paper towels to absorb the oil. Repeat until finished.

In a food processor, add garlic, onion, and peppers. Chop 10 seconds. Add eggplant, salt, and fish sauce. Chop another 8 seconds. Add scallion and ¾ of the cilantro. Turn on and off immediately. Transfer to a serving plate and sprinkle with the remaining cilantro.

Serve with rice and steamed vegetables or as a side dish with Penn's Fried Meatballs (page 99).

SERVES 2

Mashed Roasted Eggplant

JAIL MOKE MOCK KURE

When cooking eggplant, use very high heat. It cooks better with intense direct heat, otherwise some parts will stay hard and others will get soft. This dish is very healthful because it contains no fat at all. Please stick to my instructions on roasting and do not rub on oil or salt the eggplants. This is one of my paternal grandmother's favorite dishes because it has no oil.

2 medium eggplants	1 teaspoon salt
2 large hot peppers or ½ bell pepper for a non-spicy dish	2 tablespoons fish sauce (optional)
1 head garlic	½ cup chopped scallion
6 shallots or 1 medium onion, sliced	½ cup chopped cilantro

Preheat the oven on broil.

Poke the eggplants with a knife 4 times and the peppers twice.

Place eggplants, peppers, garlic, and shallots on a baking pan. (Do not oil the pan or vegetables, trust me! It will taste great.) If possible, roast it on the grill. You will get better flavor, but do not oil it either. Broil each side 15 minutes. Let cool 10 minutes.

Peel the skin off the eggplant and cut in quarters across the grain. Drain excess juice in strainer for 10 minutes. Transfer to a mixing bowl.

In a mini chopper, add peppers, garlic, and shallots. Chop 10 seconds and add it to the eggplants. Add salt and fish sauce. Mix well with a spoon. Add scallion and cilantro and mix well. Serve at room temperature with rice and steamed vegetables or as a side dish with grilled fish or chicken.

SERVES 2

Mashed Steamed Eggplant

JAIL NUNGE MOCK KURE

This dish is very healthful because it contains no fat. I make this dish when an eggplant is too small to roast. My paternal grandmother loved to make this dish with the first grown eggplants from her farm.

1 head garlic	1 teaspoon salt
6 shallots or 1 small onion, sliced	2 tablespoons fish sauce (optional)
2 large hot peppers or ¼ bell pepper for a non-spicy dish	½ cup chopped scallions
1½ pounds baby eggplants, removed stems	½ cup chopped cilantro

Place garlic and shallots in a steamer and steam 10 minutes. Poke peppers with a knife twice. Add peppers and eggplants on top of the garlic and shallots. Steam another 15 minutes and let it cool 5 minutes.

In a food processor, add garlic, shallots and peppers. Chop 10 seconds. Add eggplant and chop another 10 seconds. Add salt, fish sauce, scallion and ⅓ of the cilantro and mix well. Transfer to a serving plate and sprinkle with the remaining cilantro.

Serve at room temperature with rice and steamed vegetables or as side dish with Fish in Banana Leaves (page 172).

SERVES 2

Mashed Vegetables

SUPE PUCK

Laotians, especially women, are very creative with vegetables. In the spring, when there were many varieties of vegetables, Laotian women got together and made this dish for lunch.

½ pound green beans, cut in half or snow peas, stemmed
10 fresh button mushrooms, sliced
½ cup dried wood ear mushrooms (optional)
10 fresh shiitake mushrooms, sliced
1 cup chopped Chinese cabbage
½ pound fresh spinach, cut in half
2 large hot peppers or ½ bell pepper for a non-spicy dish

1 head garlic
6 shallots or 1 small onion, sliced
½ inch fresh ginger, peeled and sliced across the grain
¼ cup sesame seeds
1 teaspoons salt
2 tablespoons fish sauce
½ cup chopped mint
2 stalks scallions, chopped
½ cup chopped cilantro

In a steamer, add beans, and button, wood ear and shiitake mushrooms. Steam 15 minutes. Add Chinese cabbage and spinach. Steam another 10 minutes.

While the vegetables are steaming, preheat the oven to broil. Place hot peppers, garlic, and shallots on a pan. Broil 8 minutes on each side. Turn off the heat and let them sit in the oven another 10 minutes. Transfer to a mini chopper and add ginger. Chop 10 seconds.

Put sesame seeds in a frying pan and place on high heat. Shake and stir constantly until light brown, 3 minutes (they will pop and smell). Let them cool 5 minutes. Grind in coffee grinder or blender 5 seconds and set aside.

The vegetables should be cooked by now. Transfer them to a strainer and let them cool 10 minutes. Squeeze out excess water and place in a large mixing bowl. Add pepper, garlic, shallots, and ginger mixture, salt, and fish sauce. With your hands (use gloves if desired), mix and squeeze at the same time to blend all ingredients together about 10 times. Add mint, scallions, cilantro, and ¾ of the sesame seeds and mix lightly. Transfer to a serving plate and sprinkle with the remaining sesame seeds for garnish.

Serve with sticky rice or as a side dish with grilled fish or grilled chicken.

SERVES 4

Mushrooms with Fresh Dill

KORE HIT PUCK SEE

¼ cup sliced lemongrass (optional), cut across the grain	12 ounces fresh button mushrooms, quartered
1 head garlic	1 cup chopped red bell pepper
6 shallots or 1 medium onion, sliced	½ teaspoon salt
1 large hot pepper or ¼ bell pepper for a non-spicy dish	2 tablespoons fish sauce (optional)
2 tablespoons olive oil	1 cup chopped fresh dill
	2 stalks scallions, cut 1 inch long

In a mini chopper chop lemongrass, garlic, shallots, and pepper.

Heat a wok or frying pan with oil on high heat. Add lemongrass, garlic, shallot, and pepper mixture. Stir until light brown, 3 minutes. Add mushrooms, stir, and cook 3 minutes. Add red pepper, salt, and fish sauce. Stir another 2 minutes. Add dill and scallions, stir lightly, and turn off the heat.

Transfer to a serving plate and serve with rice or as a side dish with grilled pork.

SERVES 2

Roasted Mushrooms

JAIL HIT

20 ounces fresh button mushrooms	½ teaspoon salt
2 large hot peppers, poked with a knife twice, or ½ bell pepper for a non-spicy dish	2 tablespoons fish sauce (optional)
	1 stalk scallion, shopped
	½ cup chopped cilantro
1 head garlic	
6 shallots or 1 medium onion, sliced	

Preheat the oven to broil.

Place mushrooms, peppers, garlic, and shallots on a baking pan. Broil 10 minutes on each side. Turn off the oven and let it sit in the oven 10 minutes.

In the food processor, add peppers, garlic, and shallots. Chop 10 seconds. Add mushrooms, salt, and fish sauce. Chop another 5 seconds. Add scallion and cilantro and mix well with a spoon.

Serve at room temperature with rice and steamed vegetables or as a side dish with steak or grilled fish.

SERVES 2

Sautéed Cabbage

KORE GALUM

Cabbage is great for sautéing and steaming because it does not contain a lot of water. Try this great side dish.

2 tablespoons olive oil	1½ teaspoons sugar (optional)
6 cloves garlic, chopped	4 cups chopped green cabbage
3 tablespoons oyster sauce or soy sauce	

Heat a wok with oil on high heat. Add garlic and stir constantly until light brown, 2 minutes. Add oyster sauce and sugar and stir until thickened, 20 seconds. Add cabbage, stir and cook 3 minutes.

Transfer to a serving plate and serve hot with rice and hot sauce or as side dish with grilled pork.

SERVES 2

Sautéed Green Beans

KORE MOCK TORE KACK

In Laos, there were a lot of green beans and Chinese long beans (*mock tore yow*). Either one can be used for this dish.

2 tablespoons olive oil	3 tablespoons oysters sauce or soy
6 cloves garlic, chopped	sauce
1½ pounds green beans or	1½ teaspoons sugar (optional)
Chinese long beans, cut in 1-	
inch pieces or French cut	

Heat a wok with oil on high heat. Add garlic and stir constantly until light brown, 2 minutes. Add beans, oyster sauce, and sugar. Stir well 2 minutes. Cover and cook 3 minutes. Take off the cover to avoid too much water. Stir constantly until dried, 2 minutes.

Transfer to a serving plate and serve with rice and hot sauce or as side dish.

SERVES 2

Sautéed Green Beans and Mushrooms

KORE TORE HIT

2 tablespoons olive oil
6 cloves garlic, chopped
½ pound green beans, cut in 1-inch
  pieces
3 tablespoons oysters sauce or
  soy sauce

1½ teaspoons sugar (optional)
5 ounces fresh button mushrooms,
  halved or quartered
1 stalk scallion, chopped

Heat a wok with oil on high heat. Add garlic and stir constantly until light brown, 2 minutes. Add beans, oyster sauce, and sugar. Stir well until the sauce is dried, 2 minutes. Cover and cook 3 minutes. Take the cover off to avoid too much water. Add mushrooms and stir another 2 minutes. Add scallion, stir well, and turn off the heat.

Transfer to a serving plate and serve with rice and hot sauce or as side dish.

SERVES 2

Sautéed Mushrooms and Bean Sprouts

KORE HIT TORE GALK

Bean sprouts are so refreshing that I cannot resist buying them every time I go to the store.

2 tablespoons olive oil	5 ounces mushrooms, halved or
6 cloves garlic, chopped	quartered
3 tablespoons oyster sauce or	1 pound bean sprouts
soy sauce	2 stalks scallions, chopped
1½ teaspoon sugar (optional)	½ cup chopped cilantro

Heat a wok with oil on high heat. Add garlic and stir constantly until light brown, 2 minutes. Add oyster sauce and sugar, stir well until thickened, 20 seconds. Add mushrooms and stir well 3 minutes. Add sprouts and scallions. Stir well and turn off the heat. Add cilantro, stir well, and transfer to a serving plate.

Serve with rice and hot sauce or as a side dish.

SERVES 2

Sautéed Portabella

KORE HIT YICE

2 tablespoons olive oil	6 ounces portabella, sliced
6 cloves garlic, chopped	1 small white onion, chopped
3 tablespoons oyster sauce or	1 stalk scallion, chopped
soy sauce	½ cup chopped cilantro
1½ teaspoons sugar (optional)	

Heat a wok with oil on high heat. Add garlic and stir constantly until light brown, 2 minutes. Add oyster sauce and sugar, stir well until thicken, 20 seconds. Add portabella and stir constantly for 5 minutes. Add onion and stir another minute. Add scallion, stir well, and turn off the heat. Add cilantro, stir well, and transfer to a serving plate.

Serve with rice and hot sauce or as a side dish with steak.

SERVES 2

Sautéed Portabella and Tofu

KORE HIT TAO HOU

2 tablespoons olive oil	½ package (7.5 ounces) tofu, cut in
6 cloves garlic, chopped	½-inch cubes
3 tablespoons oyster sauce or soy	3 ounces portabella, sliced
sauce	2 stalks scallions, chopped
1½ teaspoons sugar (optional)	½ cup chopped cilantro

Heat a wok with oil on high heat. Add garlic and stir constantly until light brown, 2 minutes. Add oyster sauce and sugar, stir well until thickened, 20 seconds. Add tofu and portabella. Stir well and cook 5 minutes. Add scallions, stir well, and turn off the heat. Add cilantro, stir well, and transfer to a serving plate.

Serve with rice and hot sauce or as side dish.

SERVES 2

Sautéed Spinach and Mushrooms

KORE HIT SPINACH

There is no spinach in Laos, but there is a similar vegetable called *puck bong*. It is hollow and has very long stems as well as pointy leaves. Some grow in water and some grow on land. It has a lot of vitamin A. It's very cheap, especially the kind that grows in water. They grow wild in every lake and pond.

2 tablespoons olive oil	10 ounces fresh button
6 cloves garlic, chopped	mushrooms, halved or quartered
3 tablespoons oysters sauce or	1 package (10 ounces) fresh
soy sauce	spinach
1½ teaspoons sugar (optional)	

Heat a wok with oil on high heat. Add garlic and stir constantly until light brown, 2 minutes. Add oyster sauce and sugar, stir well until thickened, 20 seconds. Add mushrooms and stir to cook 3 minutes. Add spinach, stir well, and turn off the heat.

Transfer to a serving plate and serve with rice and hot sauce or as a side dish.

SERVES 2

Basil Tofu

TAO HOU BORELAPA

Tofu is not a Laotian food, it came from China. It is high in protein, so I try to use it whenever possible.

1 head garlic, chopped	1 tablespoon soy sauce
6 shallots or 1 small onion, chopped	1 tablespoon oyster sauce (optional)
	1 teaspoon sugar (optional)
1 large red hot pepper, chopped or ¼ red bell pepper for a non-spicy dish	1 cup quartered mushrooms
	1 package (15 ounces) tofu, cut in ½-inch cubes
2 tablespoons olive oil	2 stalks scallions, chopped
½ teaspoon salt	1 cup basil leaves
1 tablespoon fish sauce (optional)	

In a mini chopper, add garlic, shallots, and pepper. Chop 20 seconds.

Heat a wok or a large pan with oil on high heat. Add garlic, shallots, and pepper. Stir constantly until light brown, 2 minutes. Add salt, fish sauce, soy sauce, oyster sauce, and sugar. Stir until thickened, 20 seconds. Add mushrooms and tofu. Stir lightly 5 minutes. Add scallions, mix well, and turn off the heat. Add basil and mix well.

Transfer to a serving plate and serve with rice.

SERVES 2

Tofu with Chili Paste

TAO HOU NUM JAIL BONG

This dish is for people who like very spicy food. It is one of my favorite dishes.

2 tablespoons olive oil	1½ teaspoons sugar (optional)
6 cloves garlic, chopped	1 package (15 ounces) tofu, cut in
2 tablespoons chili paste with soy	½-inch cubes
bean oil	2 stalks scallions, chopped
½ teaspoon salt	½ cup chopped cilantro
1½ tablespoons soy sauce	

Heat a wok with oil on high heat. Add garlic and stir constantly until light brown, 2 minutes. Add chili paste, salt, soy sauce, and sugar. Stir until thickened, 20 seconds. Add tofu and stir lightly, and cook 5 minutes. Add scallions, stir well, and turn off the heat. Add cilantro, stir lightly, and transfer to a serving plate.

Serve with rice or as a side dish.

SERVES 2

Seafood

Crab with Curry Sauce

KORE POU GALI

In Laos, crabs live in the rice patties, and we only got them in rainy season. After that, they hibernated in the mud. They are half the size of a blue crab, but their flavor is unbelievable.

6 blue crabs	1 tablespoon soy sauce
2 tablespoons olive oil	1 tablespoon sugar (optional)
6 cloves garlic, chopped	1 medium white onion, sliced
1 tablespoon yellow curry powder	1 cup sliced celery
1 teaspoon salt	

Wash the crabs very well, pull apart the shells and the bodies, and break the bodies in half. You can use the shells or discard them.

Heat a wok or a pan with oil on high heat. Add garlic and stir constantly until light brown, 2 minutes. Add curry and stir well 3 seconds. Add crab, salt, soy sauce, and sugar. Stir well, cover, and cook for 5 minutes. Add onion and celery.

Stir constantly 2 minutes.

Transfer to a serving plate and serve as an appetizer.

SERVES 2

Crab with Chili Paste

KORE POU

6 blue crabs	1½ teaspoons sugar (optional)
1 tablespoon olive oil	1 small white onion, sliced
6 cloves garlic, chopped	1 cup bell pepper, sliced or 2 green
1 teaspoon salt	hot peppers, sliced
1 tablespoon fish sauce	2 stalks scallions, chopped
2 tablespoons chili paste with soy	
bean oil	

Wash the crabs very well, pull apart the shells and the bodies, and break the bodies in half. You can use the shells or discard them.

Heat a wok or pan with oil on high heat. Add garlic and stir constantly until light brown, 2 minutes. Add crabs, salt, fish sauce, chili paste, and sugar. Stir well, cover, and cook 5 minutes. Add onion and bell pepper and stir well 2 minutes. Add scallions, stir lightly, and turn off the heat.

Transfer to a serving plate and serve with rice.

SERVES 2

Crab and Seafood Sauce

NUNGE POU JAIL TALAY

1 large onion, peeled and halved	1 teaspoon salt
6 cloves garlic	12 blue crabs

In a large pot, bring 3 cups water, onion, garlic and salt to a boil on high heat. Add crabs, cover, and cook 15 minutes.

Transfer to a large serving plate and serve with Seafood Sauce (page 63) as an appetizer.

SERVES 2

Fish and Eggplant Sauce

PONE PA

1 head garlic	1 cup peeled and cubed eggplant
6 shallots or 1 small onion, sliced	½ pound red snapper fillet
3 large hot peppers or 1 large bell pepper for a non-spicy dish	1½ tablespoons fish sauce
	1 stalk scallion, chopped
½ teaspoon salt	½ cup chopped cilantro

Preheat the oven to broil. Place garlic, shallots, and peppers on a pan.

Broil 10 minutes each side.

In a medium pot add 1½ cups water and bring to a boil. Add salt and eggplant and bring to a boil. Add fish and bring to a boil. Cover and cook 5 minutes.

In a food processor, add garlic, shallots, and peppers. Chop 10 seconds.

Add eggplant, fish with broth, and fish sauce. Chop 3 seconds. Transfer to a serving bowl. Add scallion and cilantro and mix lightly.

Serve with rice and steamed vegetables.

SERVES 2

Green Curry Fish

GANG PIT PA

2 tablespoons olive oil	¼ pound green beans, cut 1 inch
1 tablespoon green curry paste	long
1 pound black fish fillet,	1 can (8 ounces) sliced bamboo
cut in 1-inch cubes	shoot
1 teaspoon salt	1 cup peeled and cubed eggplant
2 tablespoons fish sauce	2 stalks scallions, cut 1 inch long
1 tablespoon sugar (optional)	1 cup basil leaves
4 kaffir lime leaves	1 sprig basil for garnish
1 can (13.5 ounces) coconut milk	

Heat a wok or large pot with oil on high heat. Add curry and mix well for 30 seconds. Add fish and stir lightly 2 minutes. Add salt, fish sauce, sugar, and kaffir lime leaves. Stir lightly another minute, allowing the fish to absorb the flavor.

Take out the fish and leave the sauce in the wok. Add coconut milk and bring to a boil. Add beans and bamboo and stir well. Cover and cook 3 minutes. Add eggplant, stir well, and bring to a boil. Cover and cook 2 minutes.

Add the fish back, stir well, and bring to a boil. Add scallions and basil, stir lightly, and turn off the heat. Transfer to a serving bowl and garnish with a sprig of basil.

Serve with rice, iceberg lettuce, and cucumber.

SERVES 2

Fish in Banana Leaves

KNAP PA

My paternal grandmother loved this dish. She would roast it until it was dried. She would eat half and save the other half for me. There was no refrigerator, so she would reheat it every day to prevent it from going bad and leave it in a basket over the fire. That's where I always looked for food.

¼ cup sliced lemongrass, cut across the grain	½ cup chopped fresh dill
6 cloves garlic	1 pound flounder filet or 1½ pound whole black fish
3 shallots, sliced	2 pieces (12 x 12 inches each) banana leaves (optional)
1 large hot pepper, sliced or ¼ cup bell pepper for a non-spicy dish	2 pieces (12 x 12 inches each) aluminum foil (3 pieces without banana leaves)
½ teaspoon salt	
1½ tablespoons fish sauce	
1 stalk scallions, cut 1 inch long	

In a mini chopper, add lemongrass. Chop 10 seconds. Add garlic, shallots, and pepper. Chop another 10 seconds. Transfer to a large mixing bowl. Add salt, fish sauce, scallions and dill. Mix well with spoon.

Place two layers of aluminum foil on a plate. Place two layers of banana leaves on top of foil (or 3 layers of foil). Spread a spoonful of the mixture on banana leaves. Place one layer of fish on the mixture. Spoon mixture between each fish layer and on top. Wrap up both sides and ends of banana leaves and foil.

Cook on a grill 20 minutes on each side or until dried, or roast in a 375-degree oven 1 hour or until dried. You can also steam on high heat for 45 minutes.

Serve with steamed vegetables and sticky rice.

SERVES 2

Red Curry Salmon

2 tablespoons olive oil	¼ pound green beans, cut 1 inch long
1 tablespoon red curry paste	
1 pound salmon fillet, cut in 1-inch cubes	1 can (8 ounces) sliced bamboo shoot
1 teaspoon salt	1 cup peeled and cubed eggplant
2 tablespoons fish sauce	2 stalks scallions, cut 1 inch long
1 tablespoon sugar (optional)	1 cup basil leaves
4 kaffir lime leaves (optional)	1 sprig basil for garnish
1 can (13.5 ounces) coconut milk	

Heat a wok or large pot with oil on high heat. Add curry, mixing well for 30 seconds. Add fish and stir lightly 2 minutes. Add salt, fish sauce, sugar, and kaffir lime leaves. Stir lightly another minute, allowing the fish to absorb the flavor.

Take out the fish and leaving the sauce in the wok. Add coconut milk and bring to a boil. Add beans and bamboo and stir well. Cover and cook 3 minutes. Add eggplant, stir well, and bring to a boil. Cover and cook 2 minutes.

Add the fish back, stir well, and bring to a boil. Add scallions and basil, stir lightly, and turn off the heat. Transfer to a serving bowl and garnish with a sprig of basil.

Serve with rice, iceberg lettuce, and cucumber.

SERVES 2

Roasted Pepper Fish

JAIL PA

This is one of my favor dishes, because it contains a lot of aromatics and it is spicy.

1 head garlic	1 pound stripe bass fillet
6 shallots or 1 medium onion, sliced	½ teaspoon salt
3 large hot peppers poked 3 times or 1 large bell pepper, quartered for a non-spicy dish,	1½ tablespoons fish sauce
	1 stalk scallion, chopped
	½ cup chopped cilantro

Preheat the oven to broil.

Place garlic, shallots, peppers, and fish on a baking pan, and broil 10 minutes on each side. Let them sit in the oven 10 minutes.

Chop peppers and place in a food processor. Add garlic and shallots and chop 10 seconds. Add fish, salt, and fish sauce and chop 5 seconds. Add scallion and ¾ of the cilantro and mix lightly. Transfer to a serving plate and sprinkle with remaining cilantro for garnish.

Serve with sticky rice and steamed vegetables.

SERVES 2

Fried Fish

JEUNE PA

You can choose any kind of fish you like. I prefer black fish, red snapper, stripe bass, porgy, blue, snapper, and salmon.

1 pound fish fillet or 1½-pound whole fish	1 tablespoon soy sauce
6 cloves garlic, chopped	1 tablespoon oyster sauce
½ teaspoon salt	1 tablespoon sugar (optional)
1 tablespoon fish sauce	2 cups vegetable oil

Cut fish 1 inch thick widthwise and place in a resealable plastic bag. Add garlic, salt, fish sauce, soy sauce, oyster sauce and sugar. Closed the bag and let out the air. Coat the fish with the mixture by turning the bag. Refrigerate overnight or at least 2 hours.

In the morning, turn the bag over to marinate the other side all day.

Heat a large pot with oil on high heat. Add fish and fry until golden brown, 8 minutes each side.

Serve with rice, steamed vegetables, and Tomato Sauce (page 65).

SERVES 2

Fried Fish in Tomato Sauce

JEUNE PA NUM MOCK LENT

Choose any kind of fish you like. I prefer black fish, red snapper, porgy, blue, and snapper.

2 cups vegetable oil	1 small onion, chopped
1 pound fish fillet or 1½-pound	2 large ripe tomatoes, chopped
whole fish	2 tablespoons soy sauce
1 teaspoon salt	1 tablespoon sugar
3 tablespoons olive oil	2 stalks scallions, chopped
6 cloves garlic, chopped	½ cup chopped cilantro

Heat vegetable oil in a wok or nonstick frying pan on high heat. Season the fish with ½ teaspoon salt and drop it in the very hot oil. Fry each side until golden brown, 8 minutes on each side. Place on 3 layers of paper towels and keep warm.

Heat olive oil in a saucepan on high heat. Add garlic and onion and stir constantly until light brown, 3 minutes. Add ½ teaspoon salt, soy sauce, and sugar and stir well 30 seconds. Add tomatoes, stir well and bring to a boil. Cover, turn the heat to medium, and cook 5 minutes. Take the cover off and stir constantly until thickened, 3 minutes. Add ½ cup water, stir well, and bring to a boil. Add scallions and ¾ of the cilantro, stir well, and turn off the heat.

Transfer the fish to a serving plate and pour the sauce on the fish. Sprinkle with the remaining cilantro for garnish and serve with rice and sliced cucumber.

SERVES 2

Grilled Fish

PING PA

Choose any kind of fish you like. I prefer red snapper, porgy, and snapper.

2 pounds whole fish	½ teaspoon salt
¼ cup sliced lemongrass, cut across the grain	1 tablespoon fish sauce
	1 tablespoon soy sauce
6 cloves garlic	½ teaspoon ground black pepper

Clean the fish very well and pat dry. Slit the fish body on an angle ¼ inch deep, making 4 slits. Place in a plastic bag.

In a blender, add lemongrass, garlic, salt, fish sauce, soy sauce, pepper, and 2 tablespoons water. Blend 15 seconds. Pour on the fish in the bag. Close the bag and let the air out. Coat the fish with mixture by turning the bag. Refrigerate overnight and turn the bag over the next morning to marinate the other side all day.

Brush off all the excess marinates and place the fish on a fish rack. Close it tight and place on the grill. Cook each side 20 minutes.

Serve with sticky rice, steamed vegetables, and Green Pepper Sauce (page 59) or Tomato Sauce (page 65).

SERVES 2

Lobster Basil

KORE GOUNG YICE BORELAPA

It is too bad that there are no lobsters in Laos, because I love them. I have created dishes with lobster that vary from just steamed and dipped in butter.

2 tablespoons olive oil	1 teaspoon sugar (optional)
6 cloves garlic, chopped	1 can (8 ounces) sliced bamboo
1 pound lobster meat, cut in bite-	shoots
size pieces	2 green hot peppers, sliced
1/2 teaspoon salt	1 small white onion, sliced
1 1/2 teaspoons fish sauce (optional)	1 cup basil leaves
1 1/2 teaspoons soy sauce (optional)	
1 1/2 teaspoons oyster sauce	
(optional)	

Heat a wok with oil on high heat. Add garlic, stir constantly until slight brown, 2 minutes. Add lobster, stir, and cook for 2 minutes. Add salt, fish sauce, soy sauce, oyster sauce, and sugar. Stir another minute, allowing the lobster to absorb the flavor. Add bamboo shoots, hot peppers, and onion. Stir well 2 minutes and turn off the heat. Add basil leaves and stir lightly.

Transfer to a serving plate and serve with rice.

SERVES 2

Yellow Curry Lobster

GOUNG YICE GALI

1 package (1.7 ounces) cellophane noodle	1 tablespoon fish sauce
2 tablespoons olive oil	1 tablespoon soy sauce
6 cloves garlic, chopped	1 tablespoon sugar (optional)
1 tablespoon yellow curry powder	1 small white onion, sliced
1 pound lobster tail, cut in half lengthwise, shelled	1 cup chopped Chinese celery or celery leaves
½ teaspoon salt	1 celery leaf for garnish

Soak cellophane noodles in warm water for 15 minutes. Strain well and cut 4 inches long.

Heat a wok with oil on high heat. Add garlic and stir constantly until light brown, 2 minutes. Add curry and stir well 3 seconds. Add lobster and stir constantly 2 minutes. Add salt, fish sauce, soy sauce, and sugar. Stir well another minute, allowing the lobster to absorb the flavor. Add ½ cup water and bring to a boil. Add noodles and stir constantly for a minute. Add onion, stir well, and turn off the heat. Add celery and mix well.

Transfer to a serving plate and garnish with celery leaf. Serve by itself or with rice.

SERVES 2

Red Curry Lobster

GANG PIT GOUNG YICE

2 tablespoons olive oil	1 can (13.5 ounces) coconut milk
1½ tablespoons red curry paste	2 packages (1.7 ounces each)
4 lobster tails, cut in half	cellophane noodles
lengthwise, removed shells	1 stalk scallion, chopped
½ teaspoon salt	½ cup basil leaves
2 tablespoons fish sauce (optional)	1 sprig basil for garnish
1 tablespoon sugar (optional)	

Soak cellophane noodles in warm water for 15 minutes. Strain well and cut 4 inches long.

Heat a wok or a large pot with oil on high heat. Add curry paste and mix well 30 seconds. Add lobster and stir constantly for 2 minutes. Add salt, fish sauce, and sugar. Stir well another minute, allowing the lobster to absorb the flavor. Add coconut milk and stir well. Cover and cook 3 minutes.

Take out only lobster and keep warm. While the broth is still boiling, add cellophane noodles. Stir well 1 minute, as the noodles cook immediately.

Add scallion and basil. Mix well and transfer to a serving bowl.

Place the lobster on the noodles and garnish with sprig of basil. Serve by itself or with rice.

SERVES 2

Lobster in Chili Sauce

KORE GOUNG YICE

1 tablespoon olive oil	½ tablespoon sugar (optional)
6 cloves garlic, chopped	1 can (8 ounces) sliced bamboo
1 pound lobster tails, cut in half	shoots
lengthwise, removed shells	1 small white onion, sliced
½ teaspoon salt	2 stalks scallions, chopped
1½ tablespoons fish sauce	
2 tablespoons chili paste with soy	
bean oil	

Heat a wok or pan with oil on high heat. Add garlic and stir until light brown, 2 minutes. Add lobster and stir 2 minutes. Add salt, fish sauce, chili paste, and sugar. Stir another 30 seconds, allowing the lobster to absorb the flavor. Add bamboo and stir 2 minutes. Add onion and stir well 30 seconds. Add scallions, stir well, and turn off the heat.

Transfer to a serving plate and serve with rice.

SERVES 2

Lobster with Seafood Sauce

GOUNG YICE JAIL SOME TALAY

1 large onion, peeled and halved	1 teaspoon salt
6 cloves garlic	2 lobsters

In a large pot, add 3 cups water, onion, garlic, and salt and bring to a boil on high heat. Add lobsters, cover, and cook 15 minutes.

Transfer lobster to a large serving plate and serve with Seafood Sauce (page 63).

SERVES 2

Shrimp and Beef Wrap

PUN GOUNG

I love to get together with my family and have this dish in the summer when mint is growing in my sister's garden and fresh lettuce is sold at the local farm. It is more fun to have this dish with many people.

2 heads red or green leaf lettuce	6 cloves garlic, chopped
1 medium tomato, quartered and thinly sliced	½ pound lean beef, thinly sliced in bite-size pieces
1 cup bean sprouts	½ pound shrimp, peeled and cleaned
2 stalks scallions, cut 1 inch long	1 teaspoon salt
1 cup cilantro leaves	½ teaspoon ground black pepper
1 cup mint leaves	Peanut Sauce (page 60)
2 tablespoons olive oil	

Arrange the vegetables on a large platter: Place lettuce leaves around the plate. Place tomato, bean sprout, scallions, cilantro, and mint in the center and set aside.

Heat a wok with oil on high heat. Add garlic and stir until light brown, 2 minutes. Add meat and shrimp, stir, and cook to your desire, rare to medium well. Add salt and pepper, stir well, and transfer to a serving bowl.

Each person should have a dinner plate, a bowl of peanut sauce, and a small spoon. Make one bite at a time by placing one lettuce leaf on your plate. Place on the leaf one piece each of beef, shrimp, tomato, bean sprouts, scallions, cilantro, and mint. Pick up 3 sides of lettuce, leaving one side open. Spoon the sauce in the opened side and enjoy the bite.

SERVES 2

Basil Shrimp

KORE GOUNG BORELAPA

2 tablespoons olive oil	1½ teaspoons sugar (optional)
6 cloves garlic, chopped	2 green hot peppers, sliced or
1 pound shrimp, peeled and	½ bell pepper, sliced for a
cleaned	non-spicy dish
½ teaspoon salt	1 small white onion, sliced
1 tablespoon fish sauce (optional)	1 can (8 ounces) sliced bamboo
1½ teaspoons soy sauce (optional)	shoots
1½ teaspoons oyster sauce	1 cup basil leaves
(optional)	

Heat a wok or large frying pan with oil on high heat. Add garlic, stir until light brown, 2 minutes. Add shrimp and stir to cook for 2 minutes. Add salt, fish sauce, soy sauce, oyster sauce, and sugar. Stir another 30 seconds, allowing shrimp to absorb the flavor. Add bamboo, hot peppers and onion. Stir 2 minutes. Add basil, stir lightly and turn off the heat.

Transfer to a serving plate and serve with rice.

SERVES 2

Yellow Curry Shrimp

GALI GOUNG

In Laos, I could not be near celery because the smell was so strong even when cooked. It was expensive and rare because it was a new kind of vegetable, probably imported from China. It is an herb the same size as parsley. It has a lot of leaves and is used to flavor the food. When I first saw American celery, I thought my sister was tricking me until I smelled it. It was amazing to me.

1 package (1.7 ounces) cellophane noodle	1 tablespoon fish sauce
2 tablespoons olive oil	2 tablespoons soy sauce
6 cloves garlic, chopped	1 tablespoon sugar (optional)
1½ tablespoons yellow curry powder	1 medium white onion, sliced
1 pound shrimp, peeled and cleaned	1 cup chopped Chinese celery or celery leaves
½ teaspoon salt	2 stalks scallions, chopped

Soak cellophane noodles in warm water for 15 minutes. Strain well and cut 4 inches long.

Heat a wok or large pan with oil on high heat. Add garlic, stir until light brown, 2 minutes. Add curry and stir 3 seconds. Add shrimp and stir 2 minutes. Add salt, fish sauce, soy sauce, and sugar. Stir another 30 seconds, allowing the shrimp to absorb the flavor. Add cellophane noodles and stir well 2 minutes. Add onion and stir well 30 seconds. Add celery and scallion, stir well, and turn off the heat.

Transfer to a serving plate and serve by itself or with rice.

SERVES 2

Green Curry Shrimp

GANG KEO GOUNG

2 tablespoons olive oil	¼ pound green beans, cut 1 inch long
1½ tablespoons green curry paste	
1 pound extra-large shrimp, peeled and cleaned	1 can (8 ounces) sliced bamboo shoots
1 teaspoon salt	1 cup peeled and cubed eggplant
2 tablespoons fish sauce	2 stalks scallions, cut 1 inch long
1 tablespoon sugar (optional)	1 cup basil leaves
4 kaffir lime leaves	1 sprig basil for garnish
1 can (13.5 ounces) coconut milk	

Heat a wok or large pan with oil on high heat. Add curry, mixing well 30 seconds. Add shrimp and stir 2 minutes. Add salt, fish sauce, sugar, and kaffir lime leaves. Stir another 30 seconds, allowing the shrimp to absorb the flavor.

Take out the shrimp and leave the sauce in the wok. Add coconut milk and bring to a boil. Add beans and bamboo shoots. Stir well, cover, and cook 3 minutes.

Add eggplant and stir well. Cover and cook 2 minutes.

Add the shrimp back in, stir well, and bring to a boil. Add scallions and basil, stir lightly, and turn off the heat.

Transfer to a serving bowl and garnish with a sprig of basil. Serve with rice, iceberg lettuce, and cucumber.

SERVES 2

Shrimp in Roasted Garlic and Pepper Sauce

PONE GOUNG

This dish is very healthful, easy to make and taste great.

1 head garlic	1 pound shrimp, peeled and
6 shallots or 1 small onion, sliced	cleaned
2 large hot peppers or ½ bell	2 teaspoons salt
pepper for a non-spicy dish	1 stalk scallion, chopped
1 cup cubed eggplant	¼ cup chopped cilantro

Preheat the oven to broil.

On a baking pan place garlic, shallots, and pepper. Roast 10 minutes on each side.

Put 1 cup water in a medium pot and bring to a boil on high heat. Add eggplant, cover, and cook 5 minutes. Add shrimp and salt and stir well. Cover and bring to a boil and turn off the heat.

In a food processor, add garlic, shallots, and peppers. Chop 10 seconds. Add eggplant and broth. Chop another 3 seconds. Add scallion and ¾ of the cilantro. Pulse once. Transfer to a flat bowl. Place shrimp on the sauce and sprinkle with the remaining cilantro.

Serve with rice, sliced cucumber, and steamed vegetables.

SERVES 2

Pineapple Red Curry Shrimp and Scallops

GANG PIT MOCK NUT

In Laos, pineapple was available in many varieties, all very sweet. It is usually served for dessert or blended with ice for a drink, with no additional sugar needed. You can make a store-bought pineapple sweeter by placing it in a paper bag, closing it tight, and storing it in a warm place in the house for two to three days, without direct sun or heat. Shrimp and scallops go very well with pineapple.

2 tablespoons olive oil	4 kaffir lime leaves
1½ tablespoons red curry paste	1 can (13.5 ounces) coconut milk
½ pound extra large shrimp, peeled and cleaned	½ fresh pineapple, peeled and cubed
½ pound scallops	2 stalks scallions, cut 1 inch long
1 teaspoon salt	1 cup basil leaves
2 tablespoons fish sauce	1 sprig basil for garnish
1 tablespoon sugar (optional)	

Heat a wok or large pot with oil on high heat. Add curry and mix well 30 seconds. Add shrimp and scallops. Stir 2 minutes. Add salt, fish sauce, sugar, and kaffir lime leaves. Stir another 30 seconds, allowing the shrimp and scallops to absorb the flavor.

Take out the shrimp and scallops and leave the sauce in the wok. Add coconut milk and bring to a boil. Add pineapple, stir well, and cook 3 minutes. Add the shrimp and scallops back in. Stir well and bring to a boil. Add scallions and basil, stir lightly, and transfer to serving bowl.

Garnish with a sprig of basil and serve with rice, iceberg lettuce and cucumber.

SERVES 2

Steamed Fish

MOKE PA

Because there was no aluminum foil in Laos, banana leaves were used for wrapping and cooking. They add a little color and flavor to the food when cooking.

¼ cup uncooked rice	½ teaspoon salt
¼ cup sliced lemongrass, cut across the grain	1½ tablespoons fish sauce
	2 stalks scallions, chopped
1 large hot pepper, sliced, or ¼ bell pepper for a non-spicy dish	½ cup chopped dill
	4 pieces (12 x 12 inches each) banana leaves
6 cloves garlic	
3 shallots or 1 small onion, sliced	4 pieces (12 x 12 inches each) aluminum foil (6 pieces without banana leaves)
1 pound red snapper fillet, cut 1 inch widthwise	

Soak the rice in warm water for 30 minutes.

In a blender, add rice, lemongrass, and ¼ cup water. Blend 10 seconds. Add pepper, garlic, and shallots. Blend another 10 seconds.

Transfer to a large mixing bowl. Add fish, salt, fish sauce, scallions, and dill. Mix well with spoon.

Place 2 layers of aluminum foil on a plate. Place 2 layers of banana leaves on top of foil (or 3 layers of foil). Spoon half of the mixture on the center of banana leaves. Wrap up both sides and ends of banana leaves and foil. Repeat with the remaining mixture.

Steam on high heat for 45 minutes or place both packages on a baking pan and bake in 375-degree oven for 1 hour.

Serve with steamed vegetables and sticky rice.

SERVES 2

Fish Steamed in Coconut Milk

MOKE PA GATI

Banana leaves are sold at Oriental and Spanish stores. I often dream about cutting down banana leaves at my grandmother's garden in Laos.

¼ cup uncooked rice	pepper for a non-spicy dish
1 pound red snapper fillet	1 large egg
¼ cup sliced lemongrass, cut across the grain	½ teaspoon salt
	1½ tablespoons fish sauce
1 cup coconut milk	4 kaffir lime leaves, chopped
6 cloves garlic	2 stalks scallions, cut 1 inch long
3 shallots or 1 small onion, sliced	4 pieces (12 x 12 inches each)
1 large hot pepper, sliced or ¼ bell	banana leaves (optional)

Soak the rice in warm water for 30 minutes.

Cut fish in pieces 1 inch thick and 2 inches long. Place in a large mixing bowl and set aside.

In a blender, add rice, lemongrass, and coconut milk. Chop 10 seconds. Add garlic, shallots, pepper, and egg. Blend another 10 seconds. Transfer to the bowl with the fish. Add salt, fish sauce, kaffir lime leaves, and scallions and mix well with a spoon.

Place 2 pieces of banana leaves on a square baking dish and push the leaves down into the dish shape. Pour the mixture on the banana leaves and spread them out evenly. Place the remaining 2 pieces of banana leaves on top, tug them in tight, cover with foil, and tug it in tight.

Steam on high heat for 1 hour or place on a larger pan filled with 2 cups of water, and baking in 375-degree oven for 1 hour and 15 minutes.

Serve with steamed vegetables and sticky rice.

SERVES 2

Steamed Stuffed Crab

MOKE POU

¼ cup uncooked rice	1 pound ground pork
6 large crabs, shelled	½ teaspoon salt
¼ cup sliced lemongrass, cut across the grain	1½ tablespoons fish sauce (optional)
6 cloves garlic	1 stalk scallion, chopped
3 shallots or 1 small onion, sliced	½ cup chopped fresh dill
1 large hot pepper or ¼ bell pepper for a non-spicy dish	

Soak the rice in warm water for 30 minutes.

Clean the crabs, pull open the shell, and set aside.

In a blender, add rice, lemongrass, and ¼ cup water. Blend 10 seconds. Add garlic, shallot, and hot pepper. Blend another 10 seconds. Transfer to a large mixing bowl. Add pork, salt, fish sauce, scallion, and dill. Mix well with both hands, using gloves if desired. Spoon the mixture in the shells and place it on the body of the crab.

Place the crabs on a baking dish, cover with aluminum foil, and tuck in tight. Steam on high heat for 45 minutes or bake in a 375-degree oven for 1 hour.

Serve with sticky rice and steamed vegetables.

SERVES 2

Desserts

Banana Tapioca

NUM WON KOY

There are many varieties and large amounts of bananas in Laos. Their size runs from one bite to 2 pounds. Smaller ones taste better but are more expensive. There are many kinds of desserts using bananas. Traditionally, this recipe is made with a medium-size banana that has a texture similar to a plantain.

2 large ripe plantains	1 can (13.5 ounces) coconut milk
1 lemon	¾ cup sugar
½ cup tapioca	½ teaspoon salt

Peel the plantains, cut in half lengthwise, and cut widthwise in ½-inch pieces. Transfer to a large bowl. Add 4 cups of cold water, squeeze in the juice of lemon, and mix well. Let them soak for 10 minutes and strain. Steam on high heat for 15 minutes or boil for 8 minutes and drain.

In a medium pot add 3 cups of water and bring to a boil on high heat. Add tapioca, stir well, and return to a boil. Turn the heat to medium and simmer 10 minutes, stirring occasionally. Let it sit until ready to use, at least 10 minutes.

In another medium pot, add coconut milk, sugar, and salt. Bring to a boil on high heat. Add plantain and return to a boil. Drain tapioca, rinse, and drain again. Add tapioca to the pot and stir well. Bring to a boil and turn off the heat. Let it sit 20 minutes before serving.

Serve warm, at room temperature, or cold.

SERVES 6

Black Beans
in Coconut Milk

NUM WON TORE DUM

In some other cuisines, beans are part of the main meal. Laotians use beans to make dessert. I prefer to use Goya's black beans, as they cook nicely.

8 ounces dried black bean	½ teaspoon salt
1 can (13.5 ounces) coconut milk	¾ cup sugar

Wash dried beans very well. Soak in a medium pot with 4 cups warm water overnight or at least 4 hours. In the same pot with the soaking water, bring the beans to a boil, cover loosely and simmer 45 minutes or until soft. Rinse lightly and drain.

Transfer to a clean medium pot. Add coconut milk, sugar, and salt. Stir well and bring to a boil. Cover loosely and simmer 5 minutes.

Serve warm, at room temperature, or cold.

SERVES 6

Buttercup Squash Tapioca

NUM WON MOCK UR

There is only cheese squash in Laos. It looks the same as the one in America on the outside, but the inside has the same taste and texture as buttercup squash. Buttercup squash is green and smooth on the outside and is sold more at Asian and Spanish stores than in supermarkets.

1½ pound buttercup squash, peeled and cut in ½-inch cubes	½ cup tapioca
	¾ cup sugar
1 can (13.5 ounces) coconut milk	½ teaspoon salt

In a medium pot, bring 3 cups water to a boil on high heat. Add tapioca, stir well, and bring to a boil. Turn the heat to medium and simmer 10 minutes, stirring every minute. Let it sit until ready to use, as least 10 minutes. Rinse and strain before using.

In another medium pot add 2 cups water and bring to a boil. Add squash, cover, and cook on medium heat 4 minutes. Add coconut milk, sugar, and salt. Stir well and bring to a boil. Add tapioca, stir well, bring to a boil and turn off the heat. Let cool 30 minutes before serving.

Serve warm, at room temperature, or cold.

SERVES 6

Coconut Gelatin

WUNE GATI

Wune Gati is a summer dessert. It looks cool and tastes cold and light.

1 tablespoon agar-agar powder	½ teaspoon salt
1 cup sugar	1 can (13.5 ounces) coconut milk

In a large pot, mix 2½ cups cold water, agar-agar powder, sugar, and salt. Bring to a boil, turn the to medium heat, and cook until all the sugar is dissolved, 15 minutes. Add coconut milk and whisk until it returns to a boiling.

Pour into a mold or in a large tray. Let cool 4 hours and refrigerate until firm. Let it sit at room temperature 15 minutes. Cut in diamond shapes and serve.

SERVES 8

Corn Tapioca

NUM WON SALI

In Laos, corn was steamed or roasted and eaten as a snack with no salt or butter. This dessert dish was very popular when corn was in season.

3 ears fresh corn	½ teaspoon salt
¾ cup sugar	½ cup tapioca
1 can (13.5 ounces) coconut milk	

Shuck the corn and slice the kernels off the cob with a sharp knife.

In a medium pot add 3 cups water and bring to a boil on high heat. Add tapioca, stir well, and bring to a boil. Turn the heat to medium and simmer 10 minutes, stirring occasionally. Let it sit until ready to use, at least 10 minutes. Rinse and strain before using.

In another medium pot bring 2 cups water to a boil on high heat. Add corn, stir well, and bring to a boil. Cover and cook on medium heat 5 minutes. Add coconut, sugar, and salt. Stir well and bring to a boil. Add tapioca, stir well, and bring to a boil. Let cool 30 minutes before serving.

Serve warm, at room temperature, or cold.

SERVES 6

Custard in Buttercup Squash

NOY MOCK UR GATI

1 whole buttercup squash, about 2 pounds	½ cup sugar
3 extra-large eggs	½ can (6.75 ounces) coconut milk
	½ teaspoon salt

Clean the squash very well and dry with paper towels. Place squash on a paper towel. Carve the top out by cutting ½ inch away and around the stem. Slowly lift the piece up and scrape off and discarded the seeds and fiber. Save that piece, it will be used as a lid. Use a large spoon to scrape seeds and fibers out from inside the pumpkin. Place it on a baking dish.

In a blender, combine eggs, sugar, salt, and coconut milk. Blend 10 seconds and pour in the squash. Place the top back on to cover the hole. Steam on high heat 1 hour.

Let it sit 15 minutes. Discard the lid and slice from top to bottom, making a wedge 2 inches wide.

Carefully place it on serving plates and garnish with a mint sprig, slice of fruit or whipped cream.

SERVES 8

Floating Melons

LOY MOCK TANG

This dessert requires fresh coconut milk. Fresh and canned coconut milk taste slightly different. I love this dessert in the summer because it is so refreshing.

When choosing the coconut, make sure that its eyes look freshly peeled. Shake to make sure there is water inside. It should also be heavy. After getting the juice out, make sure it doesn't smell sour. This does not always mean that the coconut is bad, just don't drink the juice. Taste the meat: it should be a little sweet and have no odor at all.

½ tablespoon agar-agar powder or unflavored gelatin (optional)	2 cooked ears of corn, kernels sliced off and chilled (optional)
1½ cup sugar	1 fresh coconut
½ cantaloupe, cut into ¼-inch cubes, chilled	1 teaspoon salt
½ honeydew, cut into ¼-inch cubes, chilled	

Combine 2 cups cold water and agar-agar powder in a medium pot and mix well. Bring to a boil on medium heat and cook 5 minutes. Pour into a square tray and let cool. Refrigerate until firm and cold, 4 hours, then julienne.

In a medium pot, add 1 cup water and sugar. Heat on medium heat until sugar is dissolved and let it cool.

Combine cantaloupe, honeydew, corn, and agar-agar in a large punch bowl and keep cold in the refrigerator.

Poke through coconut eyes with a sharp tool and drain out the juice. Put the coconut in a bag and hit hard with a hammer or smack it on a cement floor until broken. Place broken coconut still in shell on cutting board. Use a small knife to lift the coconut meat from the shell. Rinse well and chop.

Continued

Transfer to a blender. Add 2 cups warm water and blend until fine, 1 minute. Place a strainer in a medium bowl and pour the coconut into the strainer. Use both hands to squeeze out the milk. Place the coconut back into the blender and repeat the same process and discard the coconut after the second time. The milk will be lighter than the first time, add salt, and mix well. Make 4 cups.

Take the fruit mixture out of the refrigerator. Add coconut milk slowly. Add sugar water and mixing well.

Add one tray of ice cubes to the mixture or serve with 1 ice cube in each bowl.

Serve cold in dessert bowls and garnish with sprigs of mint.

SERVES 12

Fried Bananas

JEUNE KOY

3 large bananas	2 cups vegetable oil
1 egg	½ cup honey
1 package (25 pieces) spring roll skins	1 tablespoon toasted sesame seeds

Peel and cut bananas in half widthwise. Quarter each half lengthwise to make 8 pieces and set aside.

Mix egg in a small bowl and set aside.

Place one spring roll skin on a large plate with one corner pointing toward you.

Brush the corner that is away from you with the egg. Place one piece of banana on the skin, fold the corner closest to you over the banana. Fold left and right sides over fruit and roll to the corner with the brushed egg. Press lightly to seal end.

Heat frying pan with oil on high heat. Drop in the banana rolls. Fry until golden brown, 3 minutes on each side. Place on paper towels to absorb the oil. Transfer to serving plates. Drizzle with honey and sprinkle with sesame seeds.

Serve hot by itself or with ice cream and whipped cream.

SERVES 6

Buttercup Squash Custard

GATI MOCK UR

3 extra-large eggs	½ can (6.75 ounces) coconut milk
½ cup sugar	2 cups shredded buttercup squash
½ teaspoon salt	

In a blender combined eggs, sugar, salt, and coconut milk, blend 10 seconds.

Line up 4 dessert bowls. Add ¼ cup shredded pumpkin to each bowl. Add egg mixture to each bowl equally. Cover each bowl with foil and tug in tight to keep steam water out. Steam on high heat for 45 minutes. Let cool 20 minutes before serving.

Serve warm by itself or with whipped cream.

SERVES 4

Red Sticky Rice

KAO NEAL DANG

1 can (13.5 ounces) coconut milk	½ teaspoon salt
¾ cup red sugar or sugar	3 cups cooked sticky rice

In a medium pot add coconut milk, sugar, and salt and bring to a boil. Add rice, stir well and bring to a boil. Turn the heat to low and stir constantly for 5 minutes.

Transfer to a round or square baking pan. Spread the rice evenly and press down. Let cool at least 2 hours and cut in diamond shapes. Garnish with a sprig of mint and serve at room temperature.

SERVES 8

Sesame Sticky Rice

KAO MUN GA

2 tablespoons sesame seeds	1 cup sugar
1½ cups sticky rice	½ teaspoon salt
1 can (13.5 ounces) coconut milk	

Soak the rice in warm water for 2 hours

In a small frying pan add sesame seeds and heat it on high heat. Stir and shake until lightly brown, 2 minutes and let cool.

In a large pot bring coconut milk to a boil. Add rice, stir constantly, and return to a boil. Add sugar and salt and stir well. Let it sit 10 minutes. Return to a boil and transfer to a square baking pan. Cover and bake in 350-degree oven for 20 minutes.

Sprinkle with sesame seeds, and serve hot.

SERVES 8

Steamed Yucca Root

This dessert requires fresh coconut milk. Fresh and canned coconut milk taste slightly different. See page 201 for tips on choosing a good coconut and removing its meat.

1½ pounds yucca root	½ teaspoon salt
1 fresh coconut	
¾ cup sugar	

Peel yucca root and chop in a food processor for 2 minutes. Transfer to large mixing bowl and set aside.

Poke through coconut eyes with a sharp tool and drain out the juice. Put the coconut in a bag and hit it hard with a hammer or smack it on a cement floor until broken. Place broken coconut still in the shell on cutting board. Use a small knife to lift the coconut meat from the shell, and rinse it well.

Grate the coconut meat with the small holes of a cheese grater, make 1 cup and set aside.

Chop the remaining coconut and transfer to a blender. Add 2 cups warm water and blend until fine, 1 minute. Place a strainer in a medium bowl and pour the coconut in the strainer. Use both hands to squeeze out the milk. Add 1½ cups fresh coconut milk to the yucca. (Blend the remaining coconut with 2 cups warm water and squeeze out lighter milk, save it in the refrigerator for another use within two days or freeze it.) Add sugar and salt and mix well.

Transfer to a square baking tray and spread it evenly. Cover with foil and steam on high heat for 45 minutes or bake in a 375-degree oven for 1 hour. Let cool to room temperature or refrigerate overnight. Cut into diamond shapes. Mix with the reserved shredded coconut to keep them separated and serve cold.

SERVES 6

Mango Sticky Rice

KAO NEAL MOCK MUANG

4 cups cooked sticky rice	¾ cup sugar
1 can (13.5 ounces) coconut milk	2 ripe mangos, peeled and sliced
½ teaspoon salt	across the grain

In a medium pot, add ¾ coconut milk, salt, and sugar. Bring to a boil on medium heat. Add rice, stir constantly and cook 5 minutes. Let it sit 5 minutes. Transfer to serving a plate and flatten it evenly. Drizzle with heated remaining coconut milk, and place mangos on top. Garnish with a sprig of mint and serve warm.

SERVES 6

Sweet Potato Tapioca

NUM WON MUN GAIL

In Laos, sweet potatoes are very small, a fourth of the size of the ones we have here, but they have better taste and texture. My maternal grandmother grew them on the sand near the river. Most of the time, they were steamed and eaten as snacks.

1½ pound sweet potatoes, peeled and cut ½-inch cubes ½ cup tapioca	1 can (13.5 ounces) coconut milk ¾ cup sugar ½ teaspoon salt

In a medium pot add 3 cups water and bring to a boil on high heat. Add tapioca, stir well, and bring to a boil. Turn the heat to medium and simmer 10 minutes, stirring every minute. Let it sit until ready to use, at least 10 minutes. Rinse and strain before using.

In another medium pot add 2 cups water and bring to boil on high heat. Add sweet potatoes and stir well. Cover and cook on medium heat 5 minutes. Add coconut milk, sugar, and salt. Stir well and bring to a boil. Add tapioca, stir well, and return to a boil. Let cool 30 minutes before serving.

Serve warm, at room temperature, or cold.

SERVES 6

Sweet Sticky Rice Custard

KAO SUNKAYA

CUSTARD:	RICE:
6 large eggs	3 cups sticky rice
1 cup sugar	1 (13.5 ounces) can coconut milk
1 teaspoon salt	½ teaspoon salt
1 can (13.5 ounces) coconut milk	

Soak the rice in warm water for 2 hours

FOR THE CUSTARD: In a blender add eggs, sugar, and salt, and blend 10 seconds. Add coconut milk and blend another 10 seconds. Transfer to a deep baking dish. Steam on high heat for 45 minutes or add 3 cups water in a large tray, place the custard tray inside and bake for 1 hour.

FOR THE RICE: Drain the rice in a bamboo steamer basket, rinse, and drain well. Fill the steamer pot with water up to 3 inches, make sure the water will not touch the bottom of the basket, and preheat on high heat. Place the rice basket on the pot. Cover and steam 20 minutes.

Heat the coconut milk in a small pot and add salt, and keep warm. Transfer rice to a large mixing bowl. Add ¼ can of coconut milk at a time. Mix well with a spoon. Let it sit 10 minutes.

Spoon ¾ cup of rice on each serving plate and spread. Spoon ¼ cup of custard on top of the rice and spread. Garnish with a sprig of mint and serve warm.

SERVES 8

Tapioca Pudding

NUM WON SCOOL

1 cup tapioca	¾ cup sugar
1 can (13.5 ounces) coconut milk	½ teaspoon salt

In a small pot add 6 cups water and bring to a boil. Add tapioca and stir well. Bring to a boil and simmer 8 minutes, stirring occasionally. Let it sit until ready to use, at least 10 minutes and strain.

In the same pot, add coconut milk, sugar, and salt. Bring to a boil on high heat.

Add tapioca, stir well, and return to a boil. Turn off the heat and let it sit 30 minutes before serving.

Serve at room temperature or cold.

SERVES 8

Taro Root Tapioca

NUM WON PEURK

In Laos, taro roots are not cheap, they don't grow well, and they are smaller. They grow organically and half of them are damaged.

My paternal grandmother grew taro roots on her farm. When I visited her in winter, we sat by the fire to keep warm. She would throw small taro roots in the fire to roast. Fifteen minutes later, she'd bring it out and opened it up for me to eat. It was a wonderful snack. I toke the big ones home to my mother to make this dish.

½ cup tapioca
1½ pound taro roots, peeled and cut in ½-inch cubes
1 can (13.5 ounces) coconut milk
1 cup sugar
½ teaspoon salt

In a medium pot add 3 cups water and bring to a boil on high heat. Add tapioca, stir well, and bring to a boil. Turn the heat to medium and simmer 10 minutes, stirring occasionally. Let it sit until ready to use, at least 10 minutes. Rinse and strain before using.

In a medium pot add 2 cups water and bring to a boil on high heat. Add taro, stir well, and return to a boil. Cover and cook on medium heat 5 minutes. Add coconut milk, sugar, and salt, stir well and bring to a boil. Add tapioca, stir well, and return to a boil. Turn off the heat and let cool 30 minutes before serving.

Serve warm, at room temperature, or cold.

SERVES 6

Mung Beans in Coconut Milk

NUM WON TAO SUAN

1½ cups mung beans	½ teaspoon salt
1 can (13.5 ounces) coconut milk	¼ cup tapioca starch or corn starch
1 cup sugar	

Soak the beans in warm water for 4 hours or overnight. Rinse, drain well and steam on high heat 15 minutes or boil on high heat 5 minutes.

In a large pot, add coconut milk, sugar, and salt. Stir well and bring to a boil on high heat. Add beans, stir well, and bring to a boil. Turn the heat to medium. Mix the starch with ½ cup water and add slowly to the beans. Stir constantly for 2 minutes. Turn off the heat and let cool 30 minutes before serving.

Serve warm or cold.

SERVES 6

Yucca Root in Coconut

SIEM MUN TONE

There is a lot of yucca root in Laos but it is seasonal. Most of the time, they are steamed and eaten as snacks. In the market, at the movie theater, and at fairs, they are roasted, pressed, dipped in coconut milk with sugar and sold as a snack. This dish was prepared for dessert and mostly made at home.

When I was very young, my paternal grandparents grew a lot of yucca. The young leaves and flowers were steamed as vegetables. The roots were thrown in the fire to be roasted and eaten as snacks. After my grandfather passed on when I was very young, my grandmother grew a little bit of everything, enough for my family to use.

1½ pounds yucca root	½ can (6.75 ounces) coconut milk
¾ cup sugar	½ teaspoon salt

Peel and cut yucca root in 2-inch-long pieces, quartered lengthwise. Steam 20 minutes.

In a large pot, add sugar and place on high heat. Caramelize the sugar until golden brown. Add yucca and stir gently until yucca coated with caramelize sugar, 3 minutes. Add coconut milk and salt. Bring to a boil on medium heat. Cover and simmer 5 minutes. Let cool 30 minutes before serving.

Serve at room temperature.

SERVES 6

Index

223

ALSO AVAILABLE
FROM HIPPOCRENE...

Lao-English/English-Lao Dictionary & Phrasebook
James Higbie
Designed for travelers and people living in Laos and northeastern Thailand, this dictionary and phrasebook features the phrases and vocabulary of modern, spoken Lao. The two-way dictionary contains over 2,500 entries; the 49-section phrasebook provides practical cultural information and the means for communication in daily life and travel-related situations. Each Lao word is romanized, and pronunciation is indicated as well. The Lao language, also called Isan, has over 15 million speakers.
2,500 ENTRIES • 206 PAGES • 3¾ x 7½ • 0-7818-0858-8 • $12.95PB • (179)

Lao Basic Course
Warren G. Yates and Souksomboun Sayasithsena
This course is designed to give students a general proficiency in conversational Lao. Short lessons introduce students to basic grammar and vocabulary while exercises reinforce newly-introduced concepts. Each section contains helpful notes on special difficulties in the language.
423 PAGES • 5½ x 8½ • 0-7818-0410-8 • $19.95PB • (470)

The Best of Regional Thai Cuisine
Chat Mingkwan
Thai people have taken the best of culinary influences from nearby countries such as China, India, Cambodia, Indonesia, Laos, Malaysia, Burma and Vietnam, and adapted them to produce distinctly Thai creations like Galangal Chicken, Green Curry Chicken, and Three Flavor Prawns.

In addition to more than 150 recipes, all adapted for the North American kitchen, Chef Mingkwan provides helpful sections on Thai spices and ingredients as well as cooking techniques.
216 PAGES • 6 x 9 • 0-7818-0880-4 • $24.95HC • (26)

All prices subject to change without prior notice. To purchase Hippocrene Books contact your local bookstore, call (718) 454-2366, visit www.hippocrenebooks.com, or write to: **HIPPOCRENE BOOKS**, 171 Madison Avenue, New York, NY 10016. Please enclose check or money order, adding $5.00 shipping (UPS) for the first book and $.50 for each additional book.